Design for Kids

Work of significance and relevance, joy and seriousness, range and depth.

Robert Venturi and Denise Scott Brown on the work of architectureisfun (2006)

Design for Kids

Sharon and Peter Exley

images
Publishing

Published in Australia in 2007 by
The Images Publishing Group Pty Ltd
ABN 89 059 734 431
6 Bastow Place, Mulgrave, Victoria 3170, Australia
Tel: +61 3 9561 5544 Fax: +61 3 9561 4860
books@imagespublishing.com
www.imagespublishing.com

Copyright © The Images Publishing Group Pty Ltd 2007
The Images Publishing Group Reference Number: 717

National Library of Australia Cataloguing-in-Publication entry:

Design for kids.

ISBN 978 1 86470 180 7.

1. Architectureisfun (Firm). 2. Architecture and children.
3. Interior decoration.

720

Edited by Robyn Beaver

Designed by The Graphic Image Studio Pty Ltd, Mulgrave, Australia
www.tgis.com.au

Digital production by Splitting Image Colour Studio Pty Ltd, Australia
Printed by Sing Cheong Printing Co. Ltd. Hong Kong

IMAGES has included on its website a page for special notices in relation
to this and our other publications.
Please visit www.imagespublishing.com

Contents

Foreword

Daniel I. Vieyra, Ph.D., AIA

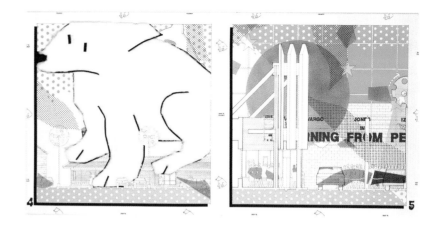

A giant 35-foot-tall dog greeted me as I joined the customary crowd of enthusiasts and curious gathered at the University of Pennsylvania for one of Steven Izenour's* famous "Learning From ..." studio reviews. Despite its overwhelming size, this dog was not dangerous but instead clearly possessed lyrical, poetic qualities. After all, the cartoon-like canine was fuzzy in texture, and soft in profile. The equally large picket fence that separated the dog from me provided comfort nonetheless. My curiosity piqued, I simply had to know what was going on in this wonderful and gigantic "front yard." The imagery belied the scheme's practicality; in fact, the "yard" was a parking lot, and the dog, the picket fence, and related symbols served to mediate between the frenetic reality of the everyday surroundings and Peter Exley's spectacularly non-heroic studio design project for a retail center. This encounter, which took place in the fall of 1988, was my introduction to Peter Exley.

This book, which chronicles Peter and Sharon Exley's practice, and the work of architectureisfun, picks up, in many ways, where the studio left off. In fact, the seeds cultivated in Steve's studio have germinated into a practice that celebrates everyday life, and, in the process, prepares children for it. In doing so, Peter and Sharon raise the bar, setting high design standards by cultivating a sense of responsibility while adding a level of poetry and fun to the practical, and the

sometimes prosaic. The Exleys' environments are at once "real and fantastic." A child who wants to be a fireman can be one; she can also be a four-legged prowling jungle animal.

The appearance of child-like innocence in architectureisfun's work is the result of sensitivity and an inclusive, participatory design process. Their environments for children are at once sophisticated and naive. Peter's captivating sketches communicate the design intentions as well as the process. These sophisticated cartoons convey the essence of the design as it evolves with input from both adults and children; in fact, Peter acknowledges that he is often inspired by children's drawings depicting their visions of architectureisfun projects as they develop.

The dramatic "Big Door" to the Dupage Children's Museum captures, in both sketch and reality, the guileless qualities of a child's drawing, and introduces contradictory dualities of scale. These at once playful and sophisticated manipulations cause children and the adults accompanying them to experience "fairytale realms" or "inverted scale realities" reminiscent of Jonathon Swift's *Gulliver's Travels*, Lewis Carroll's *Alice in Wonderland* or L. Frank Baum's *The Wizard of Oz*. The Big Door at Dupage Children's Museum or giant farm "animals" at Bonner Heritage Farm not only convey children's perceptions of the adult-scaled door to their room or their

Foreword (continued)

pet at home, but these elements also "speak" to adults, playfully giving them a view of the world from a child's perspective. These dramatic variations and dualities of scale also act as great equalizers. While certain colossal elements create a "dwarfing" sense of Gulliver's Brobdingnagian realm, cocoon-like micro environments within the interactive displays conversely give children a sense of being sheltered in a finely detailed Lilliputian realm, where, if not "giants," kids are certainly full-size people, able to play a variety of adult roles while immersed in real settings and places.

With American space often the route between two places, mobility is commonly viewed as a driving force on the landscape. Just as Dorothy's journey from the land of the diminutive Munchkins to the larger-than-life Wizard of Oz followed the yellow brick road, children in the Exleys' environments are given numerous opportunities to pursue the American passion of "moving forward" in a variety of vehicles while developing motor skills. The train, responsible for making settlement of much of the continent possible, provides the inspiration for the Winnetka Public School Nursery's Outdoor Learning Environment. More current vehicles, ranging from cars to buses and ambulances, are central to the urban environment at Playmaze at the Chicago Children's Museum. Similarly, at KidZone, children experience these real-life contexts from behind the wheel as well as engage in more active role-playing as they fuel, wash, and service their vehicles at that venerable American institution, the neighborhood gas station.

Less land-bound but equally real travel is experienced at Kids on the Fly, where the vibrancy of the airport runway is replicated in a safe setting in which, while awaiting their own flight at Chicago's O'Hare airport, a child can pilot a playfully big bulbous plane while communicating with a toy control tower that hovers above. One can also build structures, in Lego™, of course, or plan the future of the Chicago they are about to see from the sky. More exotic travel is celebrated at KidZone where a big yellow spaceship provides a glimpse of our world through big clouds.

The environments created by architectureisfun encourage fantasies and role-playing, based on the realities of place. Accordingly, these spaces echo the nature of real environments and places, ranging from the vibrant urban core and its suburbs to the natural and unspoiled wilderness and its ecosystems. The Exleys have recreated the atmosphere of the full range of landscapes in which fantasies flourish in very "real" contexts.

The energy and activity of a bustling metropolis is captured at Playmaze, with its commerce-lined streets. At downtown's edge, a suburban middle landscape of reading gardens showcases both the built and natural environments at the

Evanston Public Library Children's Library and Teen Center. Relating to both its physical and cultural contexts, the design takes its inspiration from the surrounding Prairie style architecture and features abstractions of architectural icons such as Frank Lloyd Wright's Johnson Wax building, which, reduced to its fun essentials, reinforces the message that "architecture is fun!"

The physical and social character of the Rio Grande border town of Brownsville, Texas is celebrated in a setting in which children engage in a series of activities ranging from the mundane to the sophisticated. Along its "streets," children can conduct commerce in the marketplace, prepare ethnically diverse dishes in its restaurants, or practice medicine at its health clinic. While pursuing their fantasies within "real," yet safe, contexts, children are not only given the means to role play but also to understand their surroundings and thereby develop sensibilities that will enable them to ultimately contribute toward improving their world.

The iconography of rural domesticity is given a witty twist at the Exploration Station in Bradley, Illinois. A big red barn dominates, anchoring the cartoon-like farm complex while creating a visual hierarchy that belies its dualities of scale, function, and form. While the barn, with red and white stripes on one elevation, looms large, a little "dog house" projection at the entry introduces

the scale of the child. Just beyond, a big yellow "silo" serves as a gathering point for groups; the child-like roof and bulbous form of the tower reinforce a sense of fun and whimsy.

At the Bonner Heritage Farm, we are greeted by a barnyard featuring cut-out figures of very large, very flat chickens, and their equally large, very round eggs; cut-out corn stalks that edge a very real communal garden field; and cows and their milk, in both farm jugs and containers that we might find in our grocery store. These gigantic sculptural elements, which dwarf both children and adults, make a virtue of the reality of the old farm while teaching about an everyday life that most of us know only through the end products we encounter as packaged goods at the local grocery store.

The real and the cartoon meet and support each other to teach us about our ecosystem at the Pritzker Family Zoo where we encounter both real and cut-out animals as we walk in the woods and experience nature. On an outside walk, we encounter "bears," their honey, and their habitat. We also meet otters, beavers, and "wolves." Further exploration of the woods is enabled from the Treetop Canopy, which affords a view of a natural habitat from above while climbing on abstract structural tree limbs.

Foreword (continued)

Our responsibility to the natural and man-made landscape is lyrically and literally "brought home" as we visit two families with very different attitudes toward the environment in the Stinking Truth About Garbage. This simulated landfill, itself a recycled artifact, serves as a setting in which children create treasures from trash while learning important lessons about our responsibility to the environment.

May you learn from this journey to the world of architectureisfun. The Exleys' projects, which capture the best and most basic of our everyday lives, have much to teach us. And, of course, have FUN!

*Steven Izenour (1940–2001) brought his enthusiastic and lively spirit to the practice of architecture with Robert Venturi and Denise Scott Brown at Venturi Scott Brown Associates in Philadelphia. Also with Robert Venturi and Denise Scott Brown, Steve co-authored *Learning from Las Vegas.* At the University of Pennsylvania and Yale University, Steve's studios, through his example and personality, taught young architects the importance of fun and wit in architecture. To the many he mentored and touched, both in professional and academic contexts, Steve was *sine qua non*.

Introduction

In 1994, following traditional paths in the architecture and design professions, and with a young child in tow, Sharon and Peter Exley noted a lack of advocacy for architecture with children in mind. Presented with a hands-on learning commission at the prestigious Chicago Children's Museum, they elected to craft their professional ambitions toward making meaningful, interactive places and spaces for families. Mindful to learn from both formal and informal places and historical, architectural precedents, they looked to elevate the standards of design for learning environments through the construction of new paradigms in pedagogy, play, and participatory experience through the simple implementation of good ideas.

Their firm, architectureisfun, develops architecture, interiors, exhibits, and learning resources for visionaries interested in sensorial experiences as part of daily life. Through this practice, they nurture a consciousness of design as a lifelong expectation and pursuit. Through architecture, teaching, writing, and consulting, architectureisfun creates special places that hold meaning and memory for children of *all* ages.

A unique but logical duality of the partners' roles is critical to the firm's development of its educative design philosophy, based upon pedagogies that involve, influence, and care for children and their families. The partnership can be viewed as a simple spectral range with the transient moment of experience, a learning moment at one pole, and a permanent, physical place at the other; something thoroughly architectonic. Sharon, trained as a painter and art educator, veers toward the momentary, experiential concepts; Peter, an architect, moves to the creation of "physical" environments. The reality is a complex, intertwined diagram of creativity that respects multiple perspectives, varied curricula, and an almost infinite array of developmental needs and permutations. The partners and their collaborators create multi-layered, flexible, kinetic environments that inspire intuitive and unpredictable interaction. The power of play is harnessed through architecture of complexity, familiarity, beauty, and richness.

Enjoy this work! Integrate play into your life! Architecture truly can be fun.

Play with architecture

Architecture surrounds adults and children every day, but little time, if any, is spent defining it—critically considering how the built environment affects people and how they, in turn, can affect the environment. The architectural environment is itself a work of art, both shaped by culture and shaping culture. As such, it influences human behavior, causing stimulation or suppression, generating a sense of joy or fear, and encouraging or discouraging the creative process. As such, it influences learning, as both critical tool and critical environment. Participatory architecture for children is powerful. It is democratic. As such, it creates opportunities for children to become literate co-builders of the educative design™ process. Experience can build expectation—good design as the expectation rather than the exception.

1 *The Vitruvian Kid represents every child as the child of perfect proportions*   2 *Playing with architecture*

2

Reflecting upon the participatory design process

Antoine de Saint-Exupery, author of *The Little Prince*, stated that "grown-ups never understand anything for themselves, and it is tiresome for children to be always and forever explaining things to them."

- Children understand their environments in different ways from adults.
- Children have distinct architectural needs and wants.
- Children should participate in the design process, creating critical environments that best represent their own cultural interests.
- Architects should take responsibility for advocating on behalf of and including the voice of the child.

Contemplating relevance and figuring out what's "cool" is essential and critical to the process of generating architecture for children. Avoid preconceptions and instead take an inclusive approach: collaborate with children, community, and client representatives. Nurture both the architectural and communicative processes. Educative design creates opportunities for young people and their neighborhoods to participate in decision-making, enabling them to articulate their pragmatic, developmental, and inspirational needs.

Establish a datum of childhood when beginning projects; create public forums to engage children and families, affording them equal footing. Hold collaborative workshops, asking adults to reflect nostalgically on their childhood occupations— games played, forts built, and cities imagined. Create opportunities for children to share their superb array of current vocations—some in vogue, some timeless—all of which stimulate unexpected design opportunities. Adults and children tend to reflect upon the experience of marking space, creating enclosure, changing perspectives, shifting roles, and interaction in varying degrees. Participatory involvement should continue beyond concept development and after a project opens to the public. Children should test and prototype their environments. Designers should study usage and interaction. Architecture for children should evolve; it should be flexible, and it should adapt.

Classical criteria enlightens design of family-oriented spaces

Roman architect Vitruvius advocated early cross-disciplinary study, prescribing that architects be educated and knowledgable in everything from music to medicine and astronomy to philosophy. We advocate that design is a means of putting education into practice; architects must learn about the child, respecting her ✥

3

individuality, perspective, and abilities. Designers should utilize theories about multiple intelligences, play, and learning, and refer to the potential of educational pedagogies.

Every child we design for and collaborate with is a child of perfect proportions— the ideal child. We have translated this into a classical model represented by our Vitruvian Kid™. Vitruvian concepts influence us when designing for children of all ages. Adapting Vitruvius' "firmness, commodity, and delight" into "pragmatics, developmentals, and inspirationals," we work within this balanced model. We build upon these concepts, creating participatory environments based upon design that is educated to form design that educates. That is our philosophy of Educative Design™.

4

When arranging the classical criteria in an educative and linear fashion, the *pragmatics* (schedule, access, code, budget, program, sustainability) and the *inspirationals* (exploration, interaction, wonder, awe, beauty) are the endpoints. The *developmentals* (age appropriateness, flexibility, ergonomics) hover in the center. Meandering through all three criteria, archtiectureisfun creates environments that excel within the developmental and inspirational quotients, while quietly satisfying pragmatic non-negotiable requirements. Practicing participatory design encourages the creation of non-linear experiences.

5

Architecture for children

- Is sensitive to place and experience.
- Uses relevant iconography in elegant, evocative, and intelligent (rather than gratuitous) fashion. Use gratuitous iconography where it feels just right.
- Brings education and play together—play is a child's vocation and preoccupation.
- Encourages design as expectation, rather than exception, beginning in childhood —setting the tone for a lifetime of awareness.
- Educates, referencing developmental, architectural, educational and inclusive pedagogical theories.

- **IS FUN.**

The work of architectureisfun ultimately demonstrates how we view today's child; what we create is a reflection of the cultural construct within which it is made. Designing for youth demonstrates how much we value today's child and care about her future. Designing for children is an incredible opportunity to construct "places" of collaboration and participation, indispensable for everyone's growth. Designing places that say to kids "this is a place for you," helps make kids feel safe, comfortable, welcome, and engaged. If we learn to do it right, children will know what good design is. We won't need to sell it to them; it will speak to them, educate them, and inspire them. If we design correctly, children will participate, learning firsthand how we are all part of the built environment. Nurturing children to value the environment at an early age bodes well for increasing appreciation and awareness of design as a lifelong pursuit. Creating meaningful environments that support learning, content, and fun is not a "childish" ambition. **Play with architecture. Architecture is fun.**

Architectural

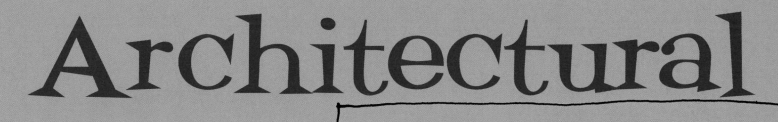

Dupage Children's Museum
Naperville, Illinois

18

The big, red, 35-foot-tall (10.6-meter) door welcomes visitors to the 44,000-square-foot (4088-square-meter) home of this non-profit institution. Emblematic of the museum's mission of opening doors to children's learning, the impressive entry also became the graphic identity. The symbolic red door is physically echoed throughout the interiors, always understood as an invitation to explore and discover.

Transforming a discarded retail lumber warehouse into a vibrant children's museum, the architecture embodies an important philosophical message: everything and everyone has value. The reuse of the building posed many challenges, including issues of structural integrity and accessibility, which were met collaboratively, creatively, and with quirky good humor. For example, the structural deficiencies required additional bracing. The resulting interior columns now reach like children's outstretched arms propping up the building in whimsical fashion. ✥

1

The impetus for the museum's design arose from face-to-face interviews conducted with children and the important adults in their lives. Children drew the museum as they envisioned it. These sketches helped identify the lively sense of color, the dramatic variations in scale, the places to reflect, the surfaces that surprise, and the ways to personalize the dynamic structure. The design team engaged in what they termed "absolute consultation," an ongoing dialogue with adults, educators, staff, and the community. The collaborative effort provided input regarding the museum's future operational, aesthetic, and design needs and led to a diversity of environment. The open layout encourages a child's independent navigation and it creates sweeping views that enable a parent's watchful eye. The referential palette moves from pulsating lime to grape to distinguish individual zones of activities. The stairs were constructed as an additional means of egress, yet they feature a charming detail. A series of etched ceramic donor tiles add recognition, color, and shine to the hallways they line.

For an institution that kindles curiosity, it is critical that the architecture meet pragmatic necessities while providing inspiration, stimulation, and an awareness of the environment. Attendance has more than doubled and more than 300,000 visitors are welcomed annually. The inviting building and its integrated exhibits directly contributed to this increase. The museum has been honored with a series of awards including an American Institute of Architects Distinguished Building Award.

Opposite *Transforming a commercial eyesore into a vibrant cultural icon*

4

5

4 *An early rendering showing the big door concept*   5 *Saving a discarded building is emblematic of the museum's educational message*
6 *Schematic design sketch*   7 *Phase 1 lobby rendering*
8 *Phase 2 building rendering*

6

7

8

10

9

11

9 A warm reception awaits children of all ages   *10 An early rendering showing building vocabulary*   *11 The brightly striped entry enables children to navigate with confidence throughout the museum*

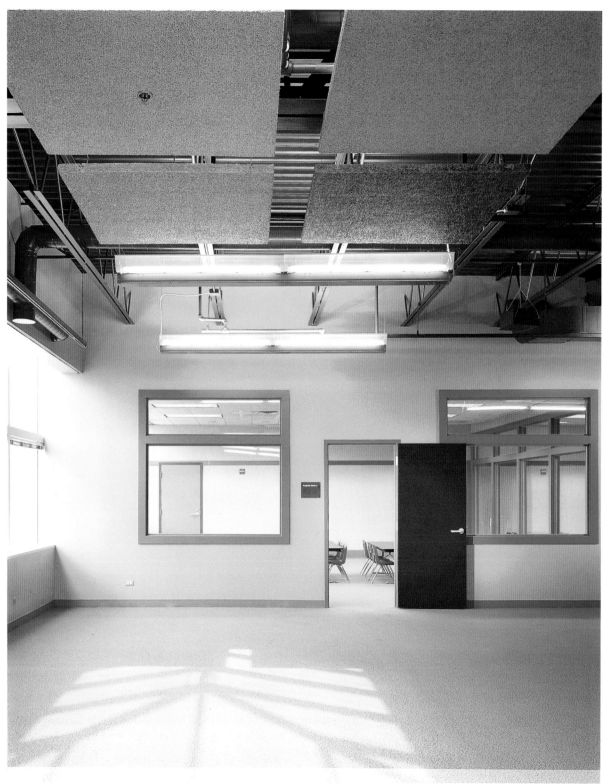

12

13

14

15

12 *Multipurpose room*   13 *Hallway "Tac-Tiles"*   14 *Schoolchildren love the KDE (kids discover engineering) labs as cool, explorative places*   15 *Interior exhibit zone*

Exploration Station Children's Museum and Community Center

Bradley, Illinois

1 Children love the "lucky charm" windows and know that this building has been designed for them   2 Tower, barn, silo, and house forms   3 The colored concrete walkway leads children and their families into this container for play and learning   4 The Exploration Station, beautifully situated on the Perry Farm, is inspired by its agrarian context

Exploration Station is a 10,000-square-foot (929-square-meter) museum inspired by the vision and spirit of this young institution and by its agrarian context. The ad hoc collection of interconnected barn structures recalls the image of the Midwestern farm but, through unexpected color combinations, whimsical windows, and a series of other details, it is clearly a container for play and learning. This impression is essential to the building being embraced by its community while being identifiable to children.

The exterior building colors are red, white, and blue—strong, patriotic colors that extend to the colored concrete walkway leading into the museum. The protruding gable, shaped like a little blue schoolhouse, signifies learning and turns into a coatroom on the inside. A yellow open-air silo that serves as the threshold provides ample room for groups to gather before entering. The color palette extends inside, with the ceiling, ducts, and bathroom tiles continuing the red and blue color scheme. Along the hallways, the windows, nicknamed *lucky charms* ⮫

2

1

5

7

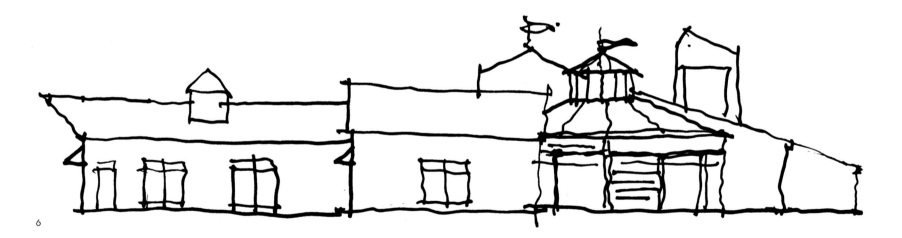

6

5 *Site model*   **6** *Elevation study*   **7** *The ad hoc interconnected barn-like structures recall the images of the Midwestern farm while providing intriguing spaces within*

8 *Tower, barn, and silo detail*

for their odd shapes, provide framed vistas. One window is purposely high, encouraging a caregiver to lift a child up to peek out into the garden beyond.

The exhibit galleries continue to reflect the agrarian spirit by providing varied, well-lit volumes with visual and physical connections to the immediate landscape and exterior play areas. The multipurpose building works as community center and children's museum, and includes three major halls for permanent and traveling exhibits, multipurpose areas, a catering kitchen, and a museum store. Each gallery provides a unique setting with natural lighting for a variety of exhibit types and experiences, including a multi-level castle with views out of the building's cupola. With caregivers in mind, there are clear lines of visibility between galleries. Interfacing the architecture of the building with the conceptual exhibit design creates a versatile and unique dynamic that functions as an integrated whole.

9

9 *Site context*   **10** *The "cut-out" reception desk greets visitors of all ages*   **11** *Children can view the museum from many places, providing them with opportunities to reflect and rest*   **12** *Visitors are immediately greeted by exhibit experiences*   **13** *The shaped windows delineate the long hallway; one is placed just out of reach so caregivers must lift their children so they can look out*

12

11

13

kidscommons

The Columbus Children's Museum Columbus, Indiana

kidscommons is unusually located in a shopping mall in downtown Columbus, Indiana. Play begins right at the storefront where children climb into the windows, putting them on display as they begin their museum adventure. This pilot museum reinterprets Columbus as a living laboratory where hands-on exploration encourages cooperative play.

The town theme reflects the city's rich resources in architecture, public art, and innovative manufacturing, welcoming visitors to this city within a city. At the *Materials Handling Center*, an assembly line complete with conveyor belt, children discover how machinery works and how cooperation enables the manufacturing process. Using recycled and industrial scrap materials, kids make felt pizzas, assemble yo-yos, or process mail. Factory aprons, coats, caps, and goggles are available in many sizes so caregiver and child can work side-by-side. Overhead a mobile of manufacturing catches the eye and frames the space. A fanciful mobile grid dangles yo-yos and other local products into view but out of reach.

1

Other work and play stations include a bubble-making
center and an enclosed safety zone for infants with soft
sculpture toys and big books. The art-making zone
is a constantly evolving mural wall of one-foot-square
paintings, collages and object fragments. Children leave
or display their masterpieces for all to view. Recycled art
materials are stored in easily accessible bins and shelves.
Throughout the museum, graphics and murals display
photographs and collectibles that highlight the industries
of Columbus. Focusing on enterprise and collaborative
work, kidscommons celebrates its community, its people
and its productivity.

1 *The museum in its mall context*   **2** *View from entry*   **3** *Reception desk at mall entry*

2

3

4

5

6

7

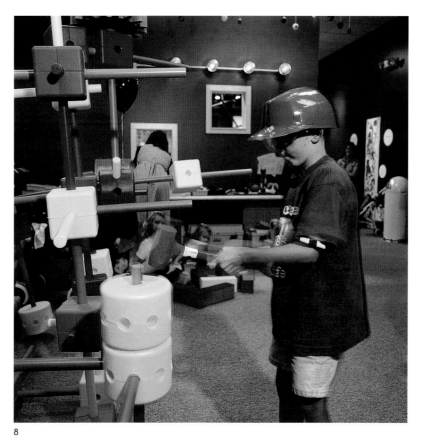

8

9   10   11   12

4,5 *Spaces configured for family learning and interaction*   **6** *Children discover the manufacturing process*   **7** *Art-making for display*   **8** *Large-scale building and architecture*
9 *Proudly displaying art*   **10** *Sharing end products*   **11** *Looking at the world*   **12** *Collaborative achievement*

The Children's Grove

Independence Grove Libertyville, Illinois

1

Independence Grove, home to the children's play area, surrounds a 115-acre (46-hectare) lake, with miles of trails for recreational activities. To supplement the manufactured standard play equipment and to help create a distinct children's zone, several new architectural elements were added. The *Entry Maze*, the *Box Bridge*, and the *Tree House* were conceived to add interest and definition; these interactive components share a vocabulary of color, taken from nature's own camouflage, and simple, box-like forms. The repeated iconography generates a sense of place that is carried throughout the *Children's Grove*, uniting the elements including the original playground.

The new entry, called *Kid's Gate*, is composed of individual 4-foot-tall (1.2-meter) metal cutouts of children applied to metal grilles. When locked, the gate appears as a line of children standing side-by-side. When unlocked, each grille pivots, creating myriad directions and forming a maze. The metal kids punched with cutout arrows suggest

2

multiple pathways, in, out, up, and through. These cutout shapes create lovely shadows on the brick pavers and frame visitors who are moving through the maze.

The *Box Bridge* is a composition of boxes and tree houses placed together in ad hoc fashion. The 20-foot (6-meter) span rises above the rock-climbing canyon, creating a place for discovery and outlook with views of the lake and the pavilion. Shaded by canopies, the box forms create charming interiors with tactile nooks and alcoves. Panels of shiny copper, rough bark, recycled plastics, chalk, and bottle caps cover the walls in folk-art style. Treasures, from skulls to pinecones, dot the interiors.

The *Tree House* presents an opportunity for visitors of all abilities and ages to be high up in the trees. Twin tree-like posts feature a series of leaves—rubberized pods encased in metal mesh nests—that create the climbing canopy. Visitors enter the climber in two ground-level locations and climb or crawl up into the cantilevered deck. Children with physical challenges can use the pulley system, which allows program staff or those with arm mobility to pull them up and into the tree house. At the top, adaptive seats move along a zip line, affording these visitors magnificent views of the river and the rare opportunity to be in the treetops.

1 *Rendering of the entry maze*   **2** *Cutout kids*   **3** *View of box bridge*

3

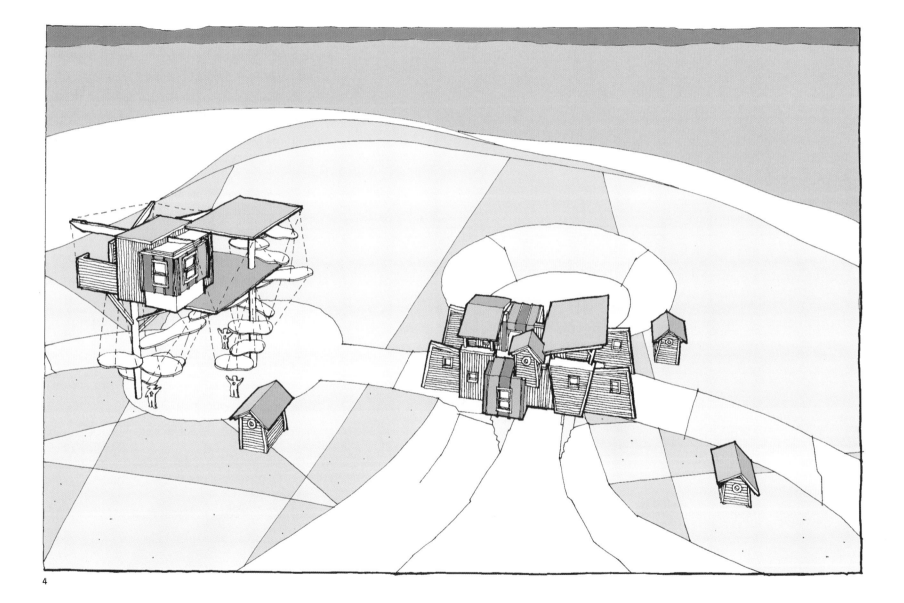

5

6

7

4 *Rendering of proposed tree house and box bridge*   **5–7** *Vistas of the box bridge*

Eastern Maine Children's Museum

Bangor, Maine

The masterplan for the start-up museum outlines opportunities for exploration and play, which incorporate state-based themes. Programmed for children aged two through twelve, the design encourages intergenerational play. The immersive environments are the central core and heart of the museum, with aspects of Maine woven into the exhibit fabric. Called "Maine Challenges," these built-in components and games link to local resources and encourage a greater understanding of the world beyond the state's borders. The program includes multipurpose rooms for birthday parties and art, administrative offices, storage, and an outdoor garden. *Around the Museum* is a floating exhibit opportunity; it uses available space as an opportunity to ignite curiosity. Hallways, bathrooms, party rooms, and even the director's door become active and engaging.

Brainstorming sessions that led to the pilot programming and design of the eight core exhibits included the perspectives of local children, the museum steering ☞

EASTERN MAINE
CHILDREN'S MUSEUM

1

1–3 *Floating exhibits permeate every corner of the museum* **4** *Rendering of "BJ," the Body Journey giant*

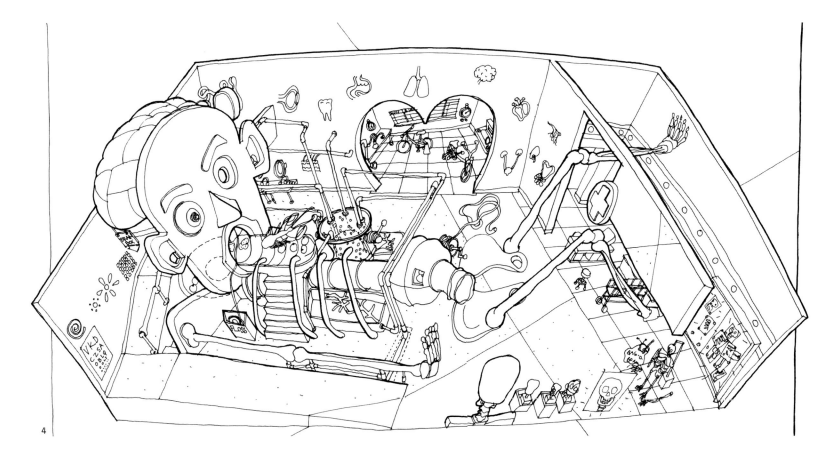

5 *Rendering of the visually animated entry*   *6,7* *Floating exhibits*   *8* *Rendering of multipurpose room*
9 *Rendering of musical exhibit concepts*   *10* *Flushing exhibit*

5

6

7

committee, educators, and concerned neighbors. Many children's book authors have strong Maine connections, therefore a literary experience was one of the first suggested. *Book Town* brings to life many favorite picture books via a series of buildings or reading nooks situated along a street. This winding trail is covered with medallions of literary honor, cut into the carpeting. Other planned environments include the *Body Journey*, designed as an enormous body playground that examines issues of health and safety, *Passports to the World,* with its four corners of interactivity exploring history, geography, commerce, and communications, and the open-ended *Texture, Light, and Color*, designed as a series of gateways or "mood rings" that tantalize the senses.

Play-based learning is highlighted in two other environments. *RiverWays* is a naturalistic experience where children go underwater, moving beneath a transparent river to discover its banks, habitats, and inhabitants. *Mechanic Mania on Mars* is a space station environment found within a drum-shaped room. Created in collaboration with the community, the interior reflects the desire to provide participatory environments for children and families of all abilities and socioeconomic backgrounds.

BIRTHDAY PARTY

8

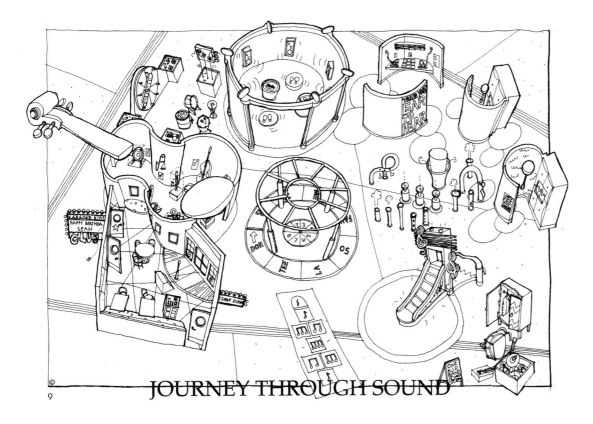

JOURNEY THROUGH SOUND

9

10

PASSPORT TO THE WORLD

11

FOUR SEASONS OF

12

11–14 *Exhibit concept renderings*

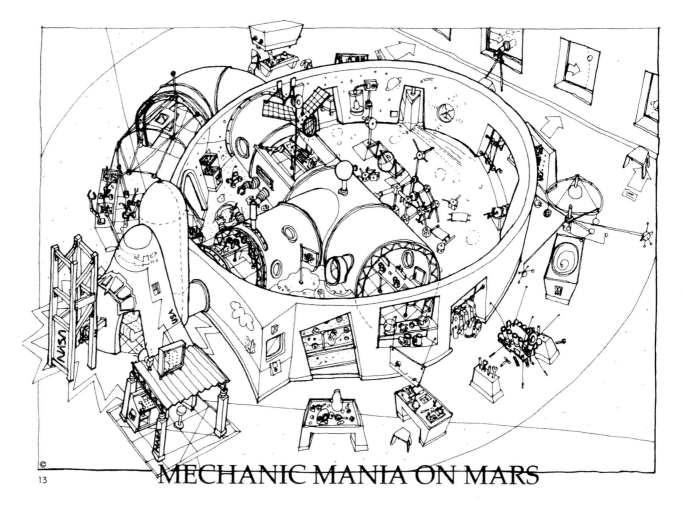

MECHANIC MANIA ON MARS

13

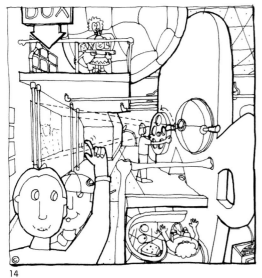

14

Mid-Michigan Children's Museum

Saginaw, Michigan

The Mid-Michigan Children's Museum is a community connector, bringing together the families of Saginaw, Bay City, and Midland in an imaginative, respectful world. Visitors driving by catch a glimpse of the interactivity housed within; the large storefront window is a place of play and wonder, adding texture and depth to the renovated building. Elements such as the walk-in window and the outdoor car painting activity highlight the museum's mission. This is clearly a hands-on destination that nurtures learning through play.

The permanent home for the museum is both centerpiece and catalyst for the downtown district's revitalization. Children's museums are unique cultural attractions, drawing more visitors than any other type of institution. This often enables them to become successful anchors for downtown or waterfront revitalization projects. The Mid-Michigan Children's Museum provides educational, artistic, and cultural experiences within an "attraction" setting, benefiting not only families within its community, but visitors as well.

1

2

The action begins right at the entry, with integrated exhibits that move visitors through the public parts of the building. Immersive environments fill 18,000 square feet (1672 square meters) of exhibit space with discovery and wonder. The impetus for many of the exhibits came directly from those invested in the museum—children, staff, educators, and community advisors helped create galleries such as *Try It*, *Night 'n Day*, and *Connections*, which foster curiosity, creativity, and caring.

The identity of the new museum is embodied in a series of iconographic cutout children that fill the multiple roles of toy, learning device, sign, logo, and threshold to exhibits and play. The sculptural kid cutouts are "dressed" with visual and interactive elements, specific to each learning gallery. Visitors of all ages are drawn to these icons of childhood, which invite children to explore, at their own pace and in their own way, a museum world designed especially for them.

3

5

4

1 *Masterplan of exhibit* **2–5** *Final design model*

8

9

The Children's Museum
Greenville, South Carolina

The Children's Museum's masterplan is a blueprint for a start-up museum exemplifying the culture of its community. The former city library building, based on Le Corbusier's *Villa Savoye*, is transformed into a composition of related systems. Taking advantage of Corbusier's *plan libre*, the layout is composed in relation to the underlying program, structural systems, enclosure, and circulation. The rhythmic arrangement of an architecturally inspired creature—a beast-like climbing wall—creates a discreet relationship between the façade and the playful interior. The beast moves inside as a climber, offering children fantastic vantage points from which to look out and into the building. The creature can be perceived as an interesting form-giving texture in and on the building, as well as a narrative, mascot-like element. Its richness comes from these layers of symbolism and meaning, and stems from the multiple perspectives that were represented during the conceptual design process.

1

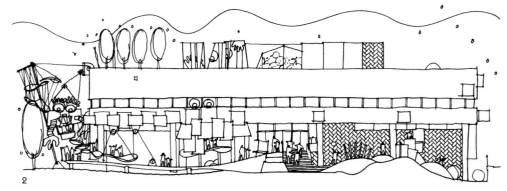

2

4

3

1 *Invigorating the entry experience*   **2** *Playing with* Villa Savoye   **3,4** *Masterplan renderings of exhibit zones*

Inspired by its upstate community, the interiors, which include 22,000 square feet (2044 square meters) of exhibit space, reflect the mountains, rivers, history, and science of Greenville through artful design. The educational exhibit goals are tied to the state learning standards, creating adventures that enhance learning and promote constructive play within developmental domains. Each adventure, from the nature-based *Reedy River Water Tables* to the lofty physics explored in *3-2-1 Blast Off*, reinforces its learning goals via a composition of hands-on journeys. The 12 exhibit zones evolved from community meetings. They present opportunities for children to find multiple ways to express themselves, from the open-ended construction of *Roxaboxen* to the technology-based television studio. Each exhibit has a strong narrative, a story that is voiced through scale, color, texture, lighting, and graphics. Additional programmed spaces within the museum include multipurpose rooms, administrative offices, and storage spaces.

5

8

6

7

10

9

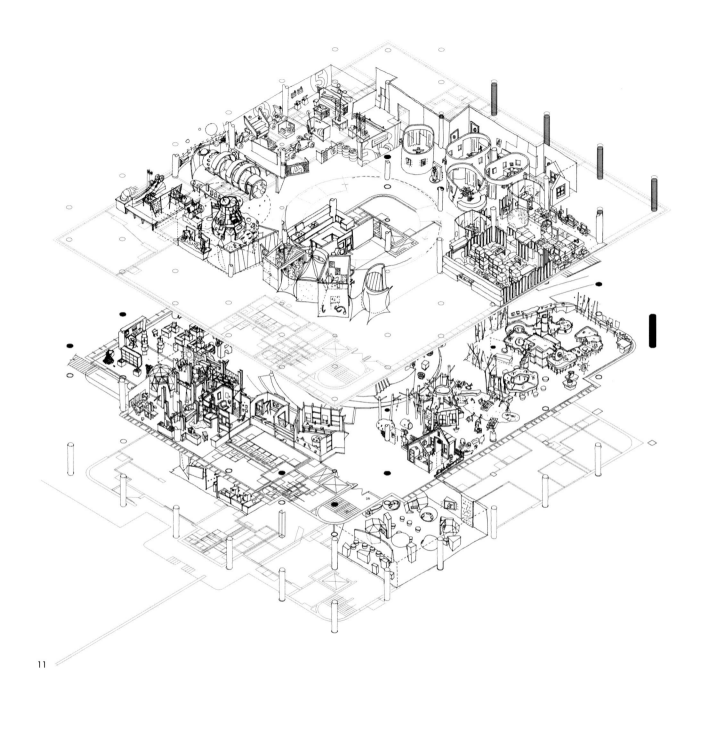

11 *Interactive drawing of the museum's three-floor layout*   **12** *Model of museum layout*

11

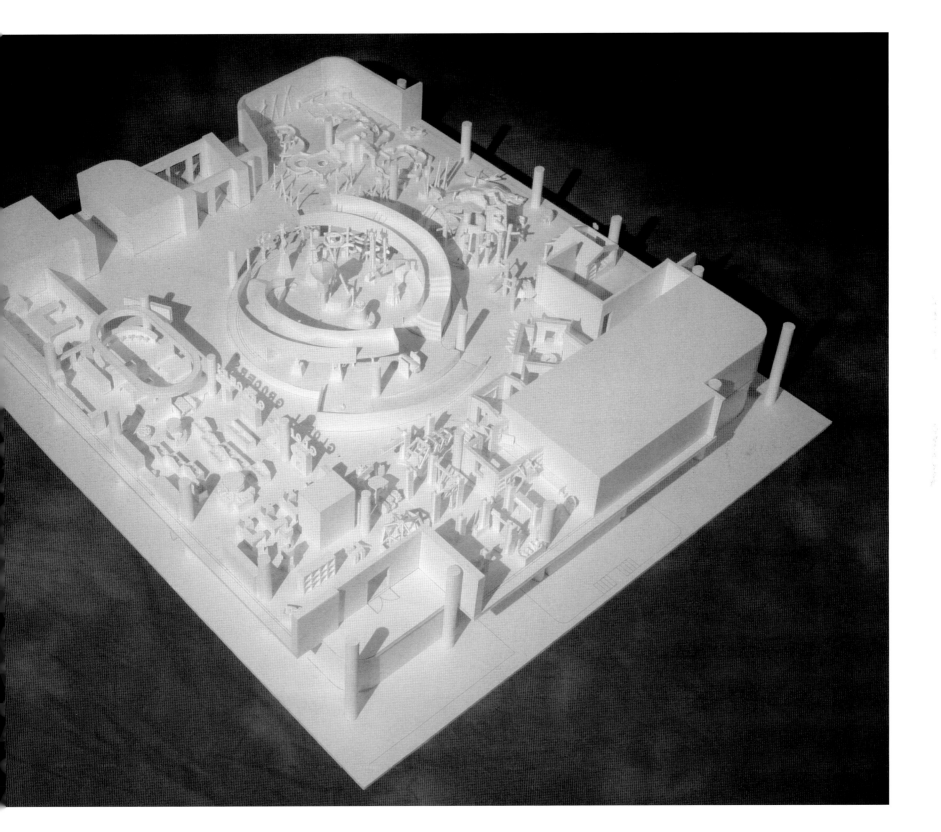

Out-of-doors

Rediscovering Nature: Kids Can Dig It

Prototypical concepts

Over the past 30 years, children have become alienated from the natural world. Many parents recall running in the woods and valleys and building secret gardens, forts, clubhouses, and tree houses, but today's child is of the electronic age, living and working indoors. Further, our culture seems to prefer the "safety" found in organized sports and typical playgrounds that offer physical challenge, yet few creative outlets. Drawing upon the research of theorists and naturalists including Richard Louv, Robin C. Moore, Rachel Carson, and Edith Cobb, architectureisfun, Inc. creates safe, exploratory, and visionary projects for children to rediscover nature in hands-on ways. A series of prototypical "gardens" and "play spaces," both indoors and outdoors, have been drafted to encourage children to develop a personal relationship with the world outside their own doors. According to recent research, increasing exposure to nature seems to reduce stress, sharpen concentration, ↳

1,2 *Imaginative atypical playgrounds offering both creative and physical challenges*

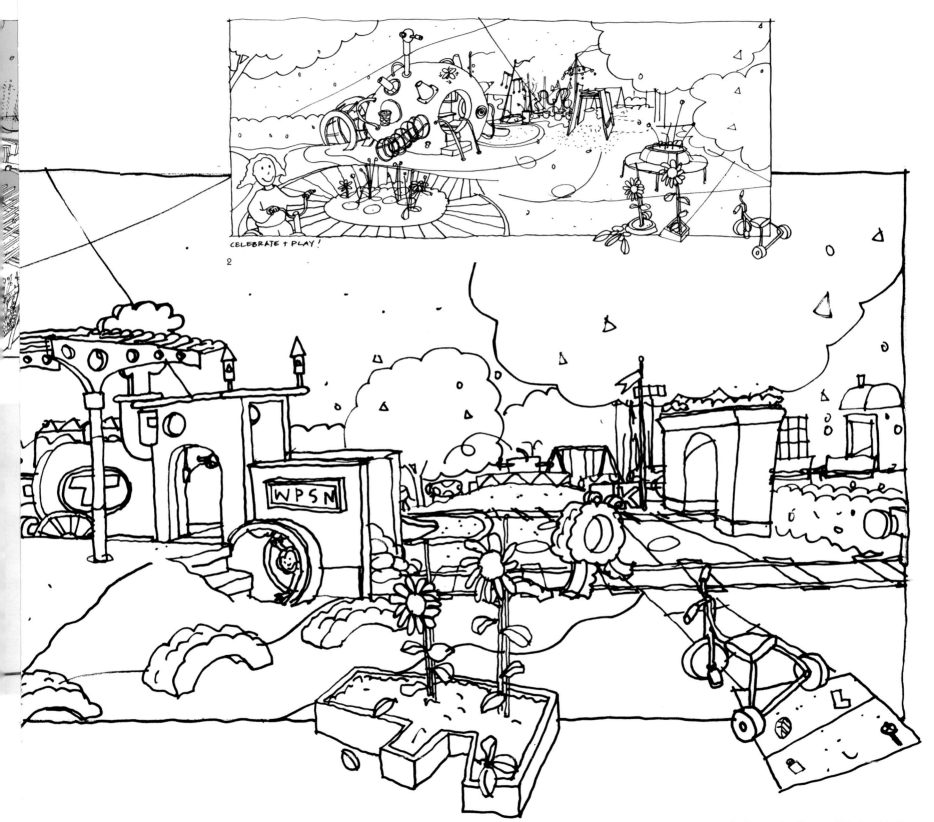

CELEBRATE + PLAY!

2

WPSN

Ogden Park Regional Playground
Chicago, Illinois

66

1

Named for William B. Ogden, the first mayor of Chicago, Ogden Park opened to the public in 1905, as one of a series of innovative park sites designed to help provide relief from tenement living. Ogden Park influenced the development of other recreational, educational, and social properties across the country. Nearly 100 years later, a major redesign was necessary to help it reconnect with its changing community. Incorporating a series of family-oriented spaces, the design encourages frequent visitation and enriches the original social programs of Daniel H. Burnham and the Olmsted brothers.

Now located across the street from a public elementary school, it was critical to create a playground and outdoor learning space conducive to after-school programs as well as the park district's summer camps. Community-based design workshops led to a program that meets adult needs and offers families a more diverse range of activities, from an open-ended storytelling quilt to barbecue grills. Children feel safe and welcomed. New play equipment 🖑

2

was installed, along with an interactive water feature that cools everyone off on hot summer days, and a canopied carousel that offers free rides for all visitors. A really big garden chair complements the classically styled fieldhouse and is perfect for storytellers or for children to climb up into. There is plenty of room to gather around, to rest, and to study the natural landscape just peeking through the opening in the storytelling quilt.

Ogden Park is an American Society of Landscape Architect's Merit Award winner for its simple, yet elegant design approach.

4 5

4,5 *A really big garden chair*   **Opposite** *Interactive water features*

Winnetka Public School Nursery Outdoor Learning Environment

Winnetka, Illinois

The Winnetka Public School Nursery's Outdoor Learning Environment takes its inspiration from trains, tracks, and stations but its philosophies from the curriculum. Striving to foster each child's potential, the outdoor environment is safe, secure, and accessible. It is a place where children are free to make choices, to become actively involved in decision-making, and to have physical and cognitive experiences out in the "open." In the classrooms, children surround themselves with rich and engaging materials. Taking that concept outside, areas such as the *Musical Forest* with wind chimes and speaker tubes, the *Infinite Loop Tricycle Path* with drive-through, the *Crazy Box* pavilion climbers, and the *Theme Gardens* with their seasonal offerings were all created to provide interest, challenge, and stimulation.

1

2

3

The Outdoor Learning Environment is an invigorated variant of more traditional, sedate (cookie-cutter) playgrounds seen the world over. The nursery's approach to early childhood education—developed in the preschools of Reggio Emilia, Italy—is based upon children building relationships. While promoting investigation and exploration, the careful arrangement of the landscape allows children to forge a relationship with nature that develops "naturally." Children can freely navigate the outdoor learning environment, without the added assistance of teachers. In fact, learning is enhanced and strengthened by a landscape that has been designed specifically for the child with its meandering path, hills for play and reflection, and areas of collaborative play. In a paradigm shift, the physical environment and natural world truly becomes the "third teacher."

1 *Sheltered threshold planting and seating area* **2** *Parade path, an "infinite loop" of activity, is perfect for tricycles and celebration* **3** *The hill, with its vista, is a place for reflection or small group play*

4,6,7 *Children navigate the playground path and its activities at their own pace* 5 *Playing with water and sand at the center of the infinite loop* 8 *Outdoor art-making and letter writing occurs naturally at pipe structures* 9 *Digging to China* 10,11 *A stage for music and noisemaking as a soundtrack for individual and group play, surrounded by the infinite loop*

5

4

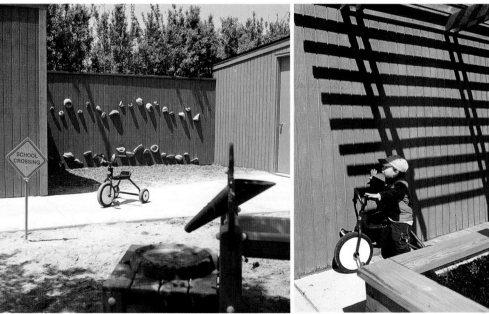

6

7

8

9

10

11

Bonner Heritage Farm
Lake County, Illinois

A 2500-pound (1134-kilogram) chicken and 14-foot-tall (4.3-meter) cow welcome visitors to Bonner Heritage Farm, located about 50 miles (80 kilometers) north of Chicago. Crafted from 1-inch-thick (2.5 centimeter) plate steel, these sculptures pair representation with presentation and bring the local forest preserves' educational programming to life. The silhouettes forge a kinship with the traditions of metal craft that were critical to everyday farm life and are left to rust within the landscape, akin to old farm machinery. As guideposts to interactive nodes, the cutouts are playful and purposeful; a benefit of their exaggerated scale is their visibility from afar that attracts those driving by.

Transforming the neglected 150-year-old family farm required an unconventional design approach. The visual aesthetic of a Midwestern farm is celebrated through the creation of engaging outdoor exhibits and the careful restoration of the 1850's farmhouse, barns, and silos. The interactive pathway and the exhibits help children

1

1,2 *Aerial view of the Bonner Heritage Farm*   **3** *Aerial detail of the community garden maze*

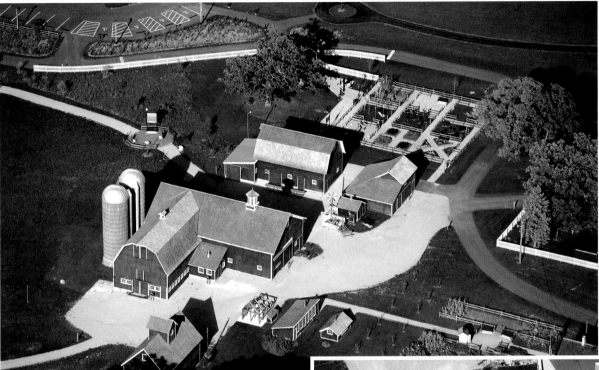

2

understand the beauty and architecture of the big barns, foster an understanding of the rigors of farming, and nurture environmental awareness. Activities include collaborative barn-raising, enabling children to raise wall panels using a pulley system, and a garden maze where kids get muddy, plant, play, and explore. Even the outhouse was restored, providing a humorous exploration of solid waste disposal in pre-plumbing eras. Accessibility, the educational message, and humor were of paramount concern and are addressed through design details and fabrication. Bonner Heritage Farm is a safe, hands-on reflection of the agrarian past with larger-than-life vitality that encourages children to visit over and over again. The Illinois Association of Museums honored the project with an Award of Excellence.

3

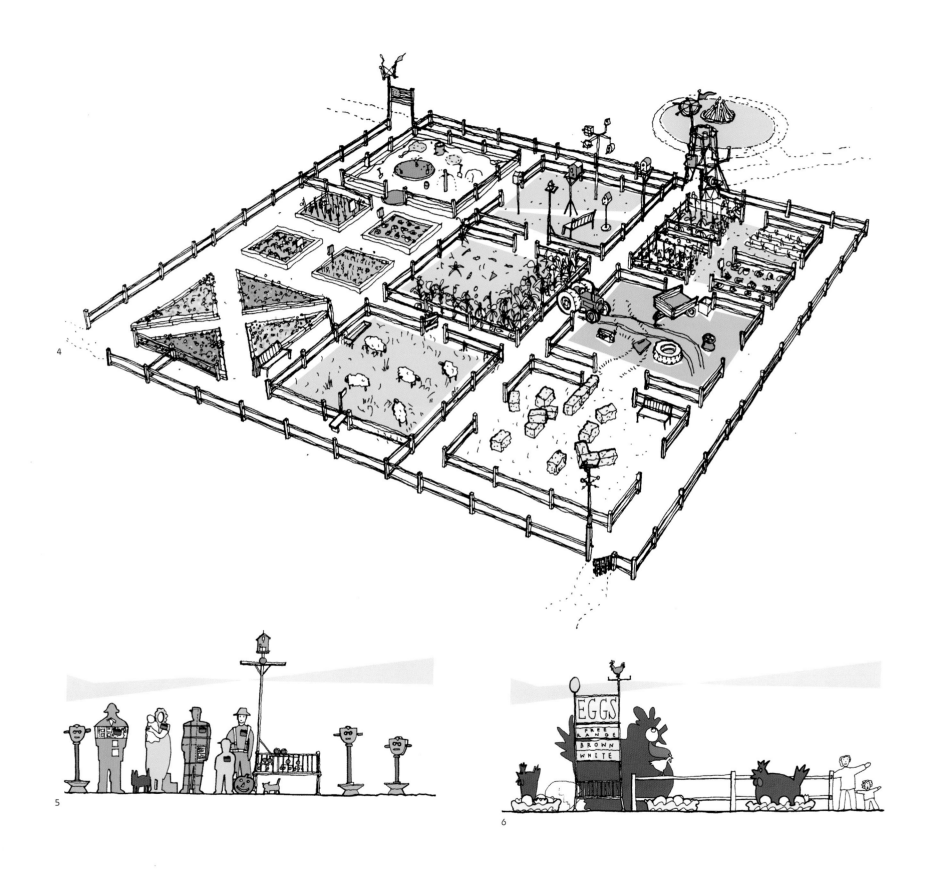

4

5

6

4 *Community garden maze with folk-art gateway sculptures and nine zones of farm-related activity*   **5** *Bonner family cutouts welcome visitors*   **6** *Oversize farm animal cutouts*

7,8 *Barn activities and programs*   **9** *Interactive pathway node*   **10** *Oversize cow cutouts with cow-pie stepping stones*

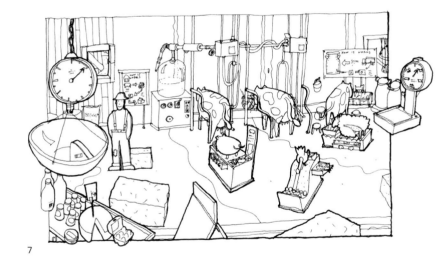

7

8

9

10

11

12

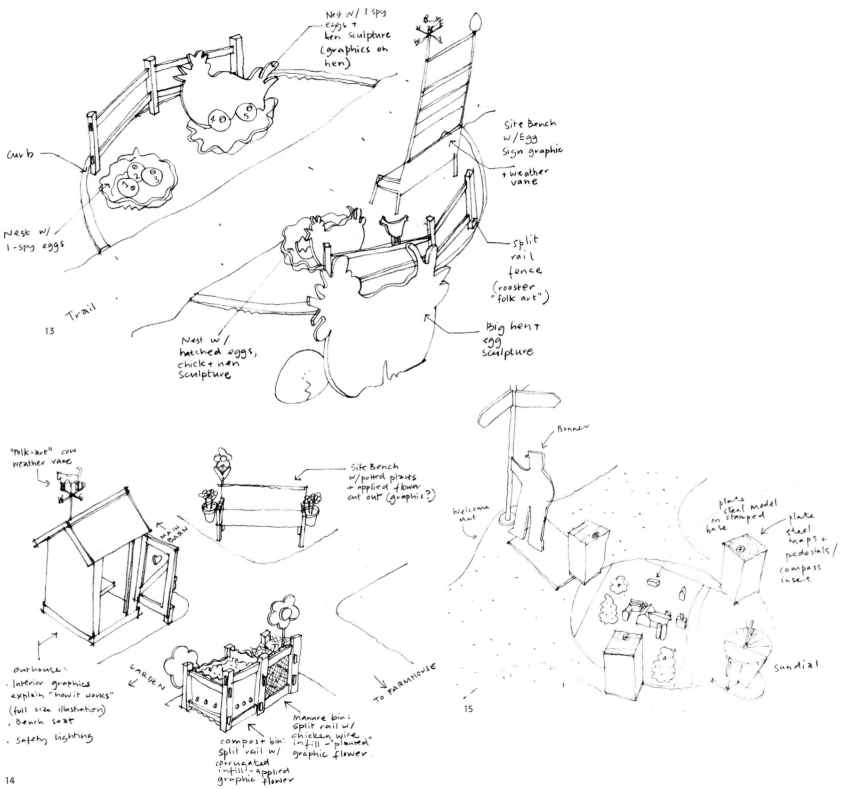

Nest w/ I spy eggs + hen sculpture (graphics on hen)

curb

Nest w/ I-spy eggs

Trail

13

Nest w/ hatched eggs, chick + hen sculpture

Site Bench w/Egg Sign graphic

+ weather vane

split rail fence (rooster "folk art")

Big hen + egg sculpture

"Folk-art" cow Weather vane

MAIN BARN

Site Bench w/potted plants + applied flower cut out (graphic?)

Bonner

Welcome Mat

plate steel model on stamped base

plate steel maps + pedestals/ compass inset

GARDEN

outhouse:
. Interior graphics explain "how it works" (full size illustration)
. Bench seat
. safety lighting

TO FARMHOUSE

15

sundial

compost bin: split rail w/ corrugated infill-applied graphic flower

manure bin: split rail w/ chicken wire infill-"planted" graphic flower

14

16

17

16 *Playing in the maze*   **17** *Raising the barn*   **18** *Testing the plumbing*   **19,20** *Milking the cows*   **21** *Meeting Mr. Bonner*

18

19

20

21

Texas A&M Math and Science Education Center at Corpus Christi

Corpus Christi, Texas

This learning facility, which houses informal, imaginative, and open-ended science and math labs for teacher training, is a departure from formal educational centers of its kind. Teachers learning to facilitate the inquiry process find that the environment is designed to physically and intellectually promote that paradigm shift—abstract thinking, discovery, and hands-on engagement are supported within the flexible spaces, indoors and outdoors.

The playful, entry pylons called *i-Beacons* create a sense of arrival and anticipation. Signifying the interactive nature of the center, the kinetic totems with their "i am" logos make empowering references. Dotting the "i" with a star acknowledges the home state and suggests imminent individual achievements. The interior science and math labs are designed as a kit-of-parts of adaptable, multipurpose furniture, equipment, and surfaces that support inquiry-based learning. Portable iQ carts feature a unique range of characteristics. Some feature sources of power, such ⬉

1

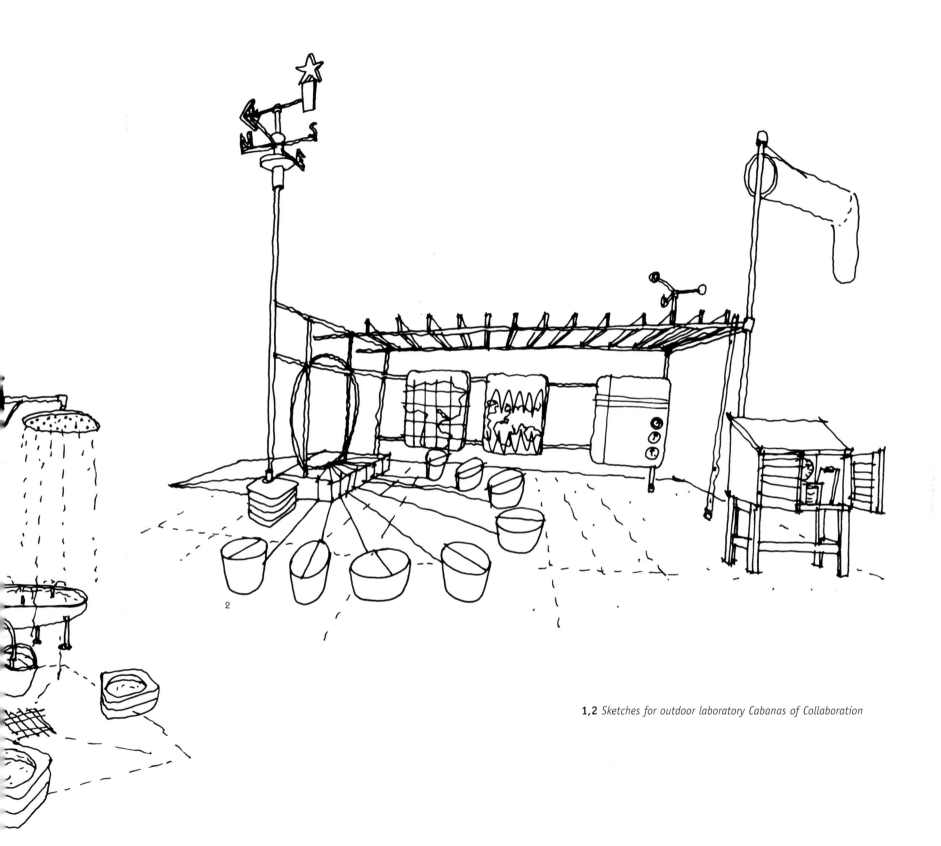

1,2 *Sketches for outdoor laboratory Cabanas of Collaboration*

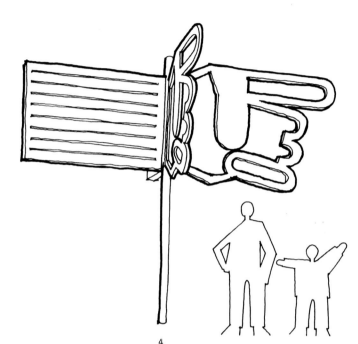

3,4 *i-Beacon sketch concepts* **5** *Indoor science and math lab* **6** *Outdoor cabana*

as wind and water, while others feature a range of surfaces, from magnetic to one clad in Lego™. The *Strata Walls* are a series of dry-erase, pin, magnetic, and tactile squares adding rhythm and activity.

Outdoor laboratory nodes, called *Cabanas of Collaboration*, provide hands-on experiences and collaborative research relating to air, soil, and water investigations for students from kindergarten to high-school age. *The Land Cabana* is an experimental garden node. A structural grid with trellis defines the space and creates shade, while its geometric spirolateral frame provides inspiration. The ground plane is also a grid, calibrated and paved so that students can modify the landscape—sorting, classifying, and arranging

plant growth. After collecting animal and plant materials from local wetlands and the bay, students can examine them at the *Water Cabana's* series of small ponds, tanks, and pumps. The third station, the *Air Cabana*, is an exploratory zone with a solar roof, fan, and pegboard bench for planting air-powered whirligigs. The modular framework at this node is inspired by da Vinci's representation of the Vitruvian Man. Children become an integral part of the trellis sundial. Standing against the frame, their shadows become the time indicator. Connecting the landscape, the individual nodes, and the facility itself are stepping-stones, using quotations from great scientific and mathematical thinkers to inspire students of all ages.

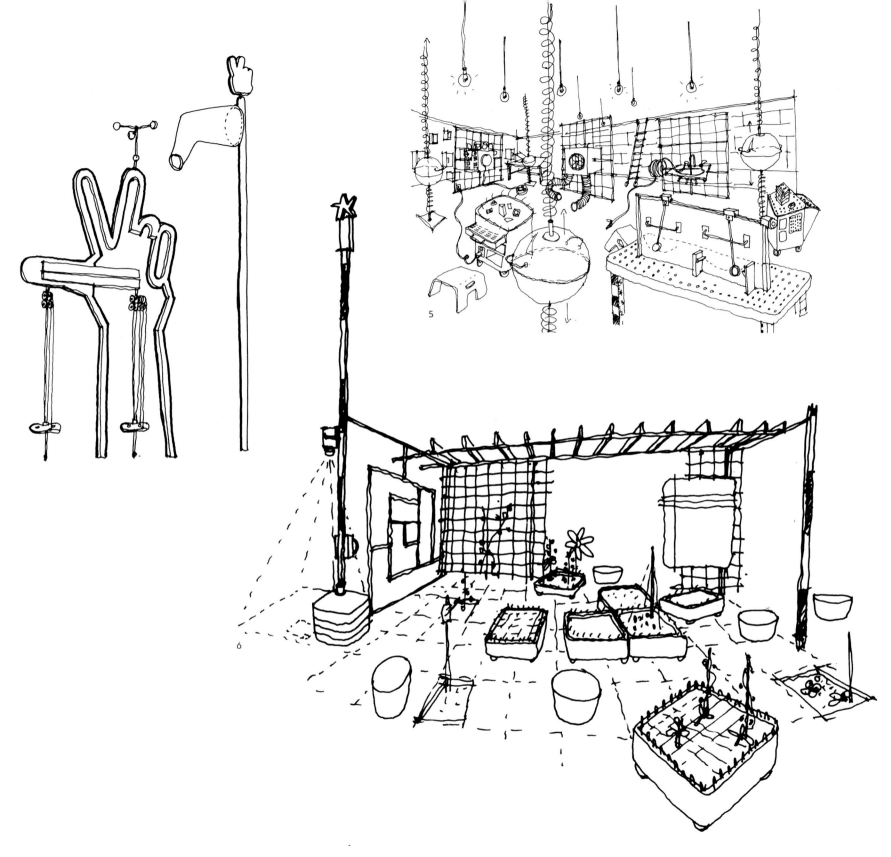

5

6

Experiential

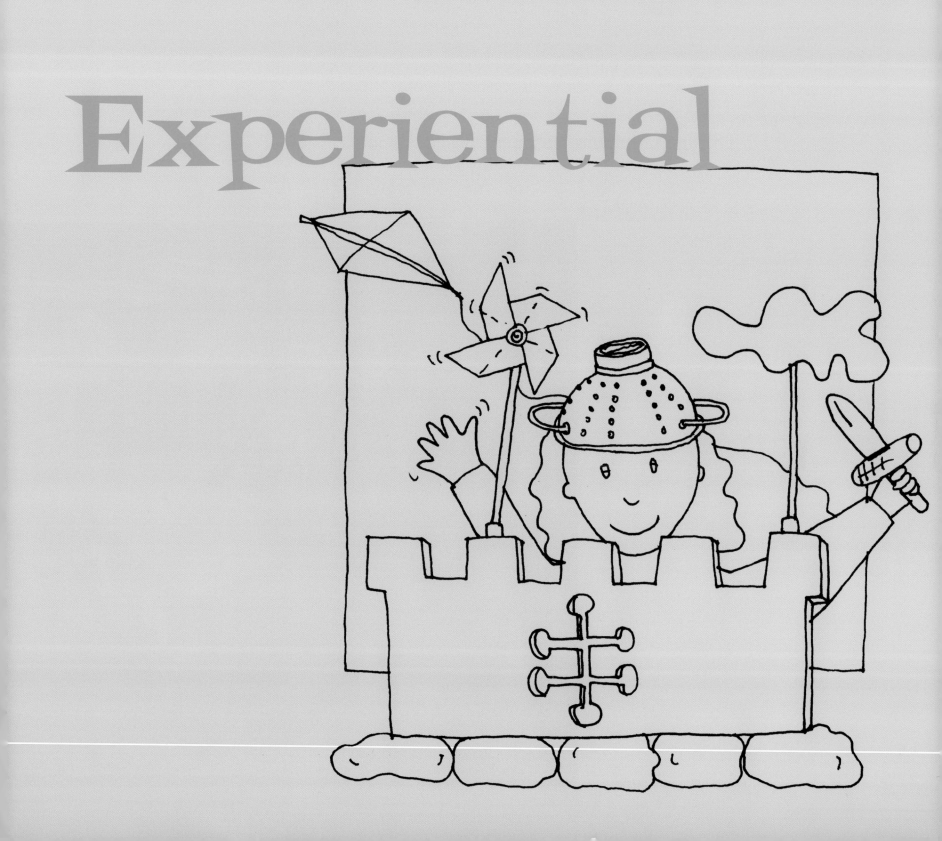

Playmaze

Chicago Children's Museum Chicago, Illinois

A fanciful metropolis, *Playmaze* encourages a child's imagination in a context-rich and integrated environment. The city in movement, work, and play beckons as the child and caregiver enter through controlled gates. This 1500-square-foot (139-square-meter) city is designed specifically for children under six years of age. Scale, proportion, color, and form create a "mini-city" that is safe while encouraging independence, physical manipulation, and investigation—all essential to a child's development.

Using the urban context as a theme, children find their way through consistent "streets" of color, materials, and floor textures that express boundary changes. When these switch, children are aware of a new zone or change in activity. Toddlers drive a replica of a city bus and sing

1 *Modes of transportation at the entrance to Playmaze*
2 *Repair shop, car wash, and gas station interactives*
3 *Young mechanics in action*   4 *Playing shop in the bakery*

1

along inside. At the car wash, they use squeegees, change tires, and apply license plates. Wearing hard hats at the construction site, children use pulleys to move building blocks around. The bakery is fully stocked for cooking, selling, and even packaging. Exploring familiar places and everyday objects helps demystify daily experiences from which children are often sheltered. Incorporating role-play and adult interaction, this carefully planned environment helps children understand their place within the world that surrounds them.

Graduated areas encourage children to perform at their own individual level of ability and inspire practicing new skills, such as crawling and climbing. The tot lot, with its "peek-a-boo" bench, offers infants and caregivers shelter and security, away from the bustle of the surrounding activity. The design of this teeming city environment included integrated software; children play on screen as they do within the exhibit, using daily city life as its inspiration.

5

6

5 *Gated entry to the mini metropolis*   **6** *The tot-lot town center*

The Stinking Truth About Garbage

Chicago Children's Museum Chicago, Illinois

The Stinking Truth About Garbage greets children and visitors with an educational and engaging exploration into environmental issues. Located in a prominent location, the exhibition is a colorful, simulated landfill. Via stimulating imagery and interactive elements, this environment teaches visitors about problems associated with disposal of solid waste, and introduces practical solutions that can be studied within the exhibit and practiced at home.

Two families with contrasting attitudes to the environment form the content while constructing the multi-sensorial space. Each family's house is a small pavilion, representative of a typical home with imagery taken from a child's perspective. Belongings and details contrast ☞

1

2

1,2 *The Green family's artful, recycled home* **Opposite** *The Waste-a-lot family's home, submerged in garbage*

the two families' habits: the *Green Family* recycles and the *Waste-A-Lots* don't. The two homes are physically and symbolically tied together via a transitional volume of garbage that makes a metamorphosis from dump to sanitary landfill to reclaimed landfill (a golf course). These iconographic elements identify the conceptual basis of the exhibit and provide an architecturally unconventional, spatial environment for exploration.

The exhibit is itself a huge piece of recycled art and architecture, constructed from trash and treasure. The folk-art façade of reclaimed possessions is fanciful and informative, covered in smiling brooms, vinyl record albums, and bits and pieces of early technologies. Children turn trash into treasure as they make art in the exhibit's *Re-Creation Station*. To test their newfound environmental knowledge, children play the interactive computer program, illustrated and developed alongside the exhibit. Young visitors and their families learn to reduce, reuse, and recreate while they discover the *Stinking Truth About Garbage*.

4 *Learning about how much trash you make*   5 *Entering The Stinking Truth About Garbage, preparing to uncover creative "green" solutions*   6 *Understand first the problems of waste, then turn trash into treasures*   7 *The fanciful folk-art façade*

6   7

Medieval Castle

Exploration Station Children's Museum Bourbonnais, Illinois

1 Rendering of castle 2 View of castle façade 3,4 Concept and activity development sketches

Children step back in time at the Medieval Castle, a famous, infamous, and unique two-story environment that enchants visitors of all ages. Entering through a gated front complete with drawbridge, children are captivated by the innards of the castle. Moving from room to room and from floor to floor, children and caregivers explore the dungeon with its rats and chains, the battlements, and the throne room where anyone can be king for the day. Many enjoy utilizing their navigational skills to help them find their way to the banquet room where full feasts can be set out and secret passageways can be discovered. Acting out their fantasies, children can don jester's hats and entertain the royal family under the striped tent. Or they can present a show at the puppet theatre, choosing puppets including hawks, horses, and mystical beasts.

The Medieval Castle features a climbing tower that allows children to ignite their imaginations. Venturing upward to the periscope room, children peer out of the windows

1

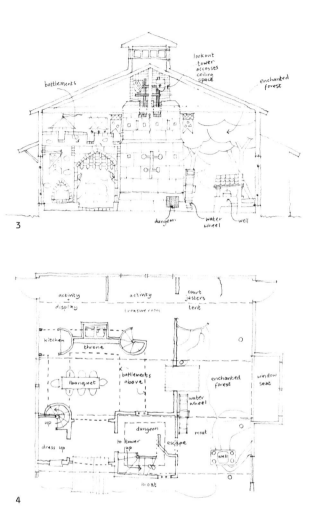

3

4

of the building's cupola to capture real views of the nature trails outside. Books, manuscripts, and costumes are found throughout the castle, encouraging the connection of history and literature. With its multitude of timeless experiences, turrets, and tunnels, the Medieval Castle is a great place to be a knight, a damsel in distress, or just a kid—or to feel like one.

2

KidZone

Louisville Science Center Louisville, Kentucky

1

Children are natural scientists, experts at using play to experiment, discover, and inquire. Vehicles of exploration—the city bus, the two-story airplane, the ambulance, and the spaceship—are designed to incorporate role-playing and dramatic play, as well as providing zones for science-based learning. The Louisville city bus, scaled appropriately for children, features authentic seats and a fare machine. Pretending to be the passenger or the driver, young visitors role-play by consulting the iconographic maps, changing the license plates, and driving the bus. In the emergency zone, children steer the ambulance and care for the patient riding in the back. "Take Action" signs throughout the exhibit transmit messages; in this emergency zone the lesson is how to "call 911." By practicing elements of daily life, children feel more confident and capable. ☜

1 *Using forces for early learning construction experiences* **2** *Street carts for sharing science with young learners*
Opposite *Familiar and lively streetscape entry*

2

Each vehicle is located within an appropriate environment: the plane is in the clouds and the bus is on a crowded city street. Surrounding the neighborhood is a series of street carts with brightly colored, striped canopies. A changing array of "merchandise" is designed to make each vendor unique; children engage in dramatic play with puppets, constructive play with blocks, and artistic play using light boxes. The big, yellow airplane has climbing passages that lead young aviators to the cockpit where they can radio the control tower or to the galley, where they can prepare lunch. Sliding right out of the back of the plane, young travelers descend to the cargo area back on Main Street. Across the road, a spaceship has landed. Inside is an intimate nook where caregivers and children sit together to read. The lunar module has plenty of windows for viewing the stars and moons, many of which orbit above the nearby pre-walker zone. Babies crawl, touch, and enjoy their own tactile, padded moonscape. At the construction zone, children don hard hats and operate dump trucks while experimenting with pulleys, magnets, and fulcrums. With a view of the Ohio River, kids get wet at the water table while exploring the properties of water. The water table features several levels for circulating water, places to dam it up, and boats and fish to move about.

KidZone, with its themed environments, is a playful, hands-on scientific cityscape for children and their caregivers.

4 Jetting through the sky on the multi-level airplane of discovery   *5 Flying in quiet space within the lunar module*   *6 Sinking and floating activities at the water table*
7 Experimenting together with light and color at the illuminated street cart   *8 Exploring worlds of science*

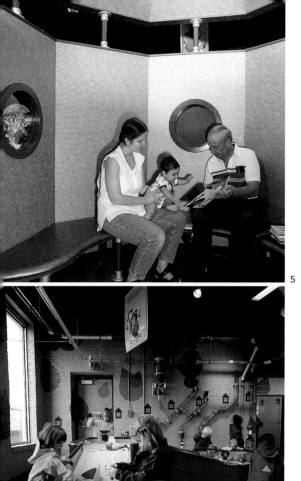

5

6

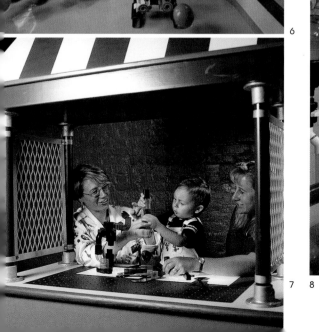

7 8

My Museum

Chicago Children's Museum Chicago, Illinois

My Museum is designed to create hands-on opportunities for personal and interpersonal expression and exploration. The body-scaled, three-dimensional entry letters entice visitors into a previously underutilized exhibit hall. Spelling out "My Museum" in various ways using tactile and diverse materials, the letters represent playful and creative ways to communicate. The environment is intentionally left unfinished and changeable, so that visitors not only interact, but also create the space around them.

Children engage in art-making using both traditional and innovative materials. At the letters, for example, children chalk on the "u", tack drawings up on the "s", and walk right through the "e" linen portal. Each letter provides ☞

1 *Entry communicates the importance of expressive action in a big way*   2 *Forming identity in clay*   3 *Reflecting sense of self*   4 *Sharing notions of one another*

1

What do you like most

5–7 *Navigating around My Museum*

7

6

10

either storage or a creative surface on which artwork, messages, and more are applied. The museum letters become an ever-changing landscape. Nearby art-making stations include a clay bust interactive where children work side by side, exploring their own likenesses and a Plexiglas interactive where visitors paint each other on full-size child cutouts. *Kaleidoscope for Kids* is a tubular mini-environment lined with mirrors for the youngest of artists.

A photo booth captures children's images along with personal messages. Kids chalk a caption for their self-portrait and then insert a portrait into the neighborhood mural. Styled after local artist Roger Brown's engaging, populated cityscapes, these murals create an instantaneous, growing sense of community within the gallery. Located just behind the museum letters is a display of children's art, collaborative art-making experiences, and community outreach artwork. A second tier of artwork, hung just below the picture rail, is positioned at the crawl-through level. These black and white photographs and paintings are created especially for infants to view. Children and caregivers can easily put the art they created on display; the front-loading framing is easily accessible. All of the artwork, permanent, instant, and temporary, is hung and curated in sophisticated, "adult" ways, from Victorian-style oval portrait frames to a series of acrylic display cases for clay creations. This encourages visitors of all ages to view children's art respectfully. *My Museum* was designed to embody its philosophical message, that art created from self-expression is valued. This authentic gallery experience helps build self-awareness and nurtures openness toward others.

8 *Capturing personal expression*   **9** *Placing personal expression within the community mural*   **10** *Viewing personal expressions exhibited within My Museum's formal gallery*

Adventure With Babar, King of the Elephants

Chicago Children's Museum Chicago, Illinois

The design is inspired by the heartwarming stories of the classic tales by Laurent de Brunhoff. Nostalgic snapshots of Babar's travels are transformed into immersive, referential environments that transport children between the ages of three and eight, and their families, to places of adventure. Like a gigantic picture postcard come to life, colorful, glowing letters spell out "Babar" while defining the entry and welcoming visitors.

Just beyond the entry, giant travel trunks, filled with elephant-sized belongings, lead children into Babar's park. The merry-go-round presents all of Babar's famous modes of transportation, from the red convertible to the yellow hot air balloon. Children can dress up as book characters, a train conductor, or an artist. Many children will notice that the grillwork at the art nouveau-inspired ticket booth resembles the gentle elephant's profile. The author tried to employ a device, with elements that resembled Babar, within the stories for children to find. Within the exhibit, that concept was utilized ⮫

1

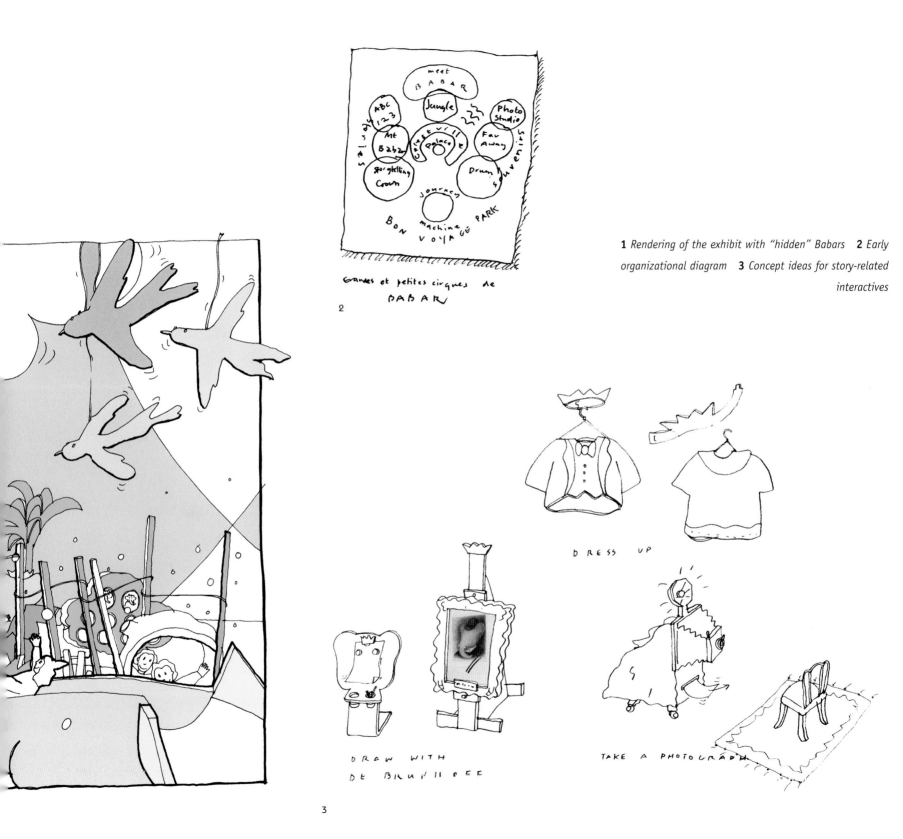

Grandes et petites cirques de
BABAR

2

1 *Rendering of the exhibit with "hidden" Babars* 2 *Early organizational diagram* 3 *Concept ideas for story-related interactives*

DRESS UP

DRAW WITH
DE BRUNHOFF

TAKE A PHOTOGRAPH

3

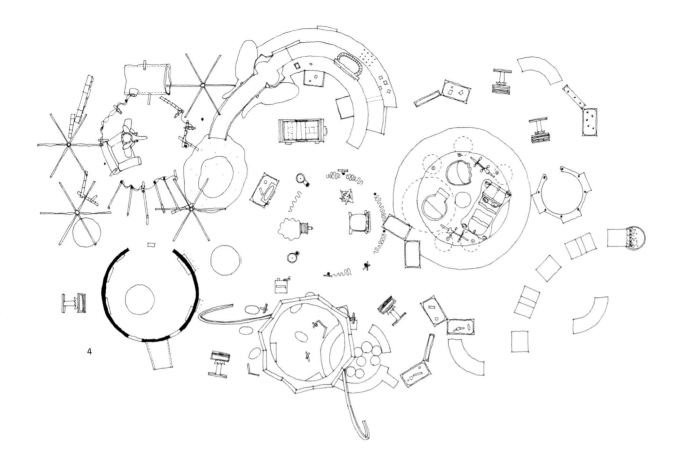

4 *Plan layout option* 5 *Rendering of overall exhibit*

architecturally. A portal is shaped as if the elephant king just walked through it. The storytelling area resembles a large, suspended metal crown, its two dangling globes looking like Babar's eyes. Additional activity areas where Babar can be found in one form or another include art-making, photography, preschool, and within the gallery of the real artwork.

During the concept development sessions with children, physical adventure was mentioned as an important element in Babar's travels. The design solution included a jungle-like maze filled with bodily kinesthetic challenges, including climbing, swinging, and balancing. Soft sculpture vines create the density of the forest, which then opens up into a clearing in the woods. Babar ↰

5

Alice in Wonderland Play Space

Young at Art Children's Museum Davie, Florida

Brightly colored and spatially stimulating, this wonderland is artist Deloss McGraw's personal vision of Alice, designed as an early childhood place of play. Within an undulating ribbon of curved walls, children discover a keyhole portal to the *Alice in Wonderland Play Space*. In a unique collaboration, the artist and the design team worked together, creating a bright, invigorated palette and an environment filled with recycled, tactile materials.

Alice's Down the Rabbit Hole, an irresistible entry art piece, is engaging and interactive. Preschoolers enter, using their own bodies to investigate its form and use. Fiber optics line the interior, creating an atmosphere of light and changing color, keeping the tunnel cozy. Children use their "body smarts" to move through the rabbit hole and then do it all over again.

Alice's Pool of Tears is a series of connecting, small water tables that keep the normally exuberant water experience intimate and peaceful. Versions of Alice's face spout

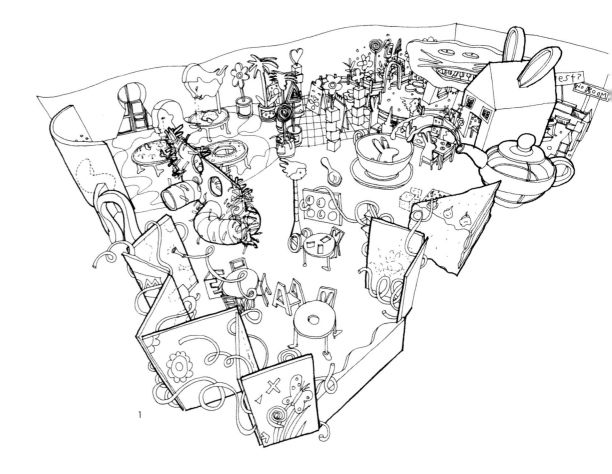

1

cascading fountains of tear-like water. Ripple pop-ups encourage children to "swim" by popping up underneath in the acrylic domes with Alice and her friends. Children and caregivers relax while pouring, sifting, splashing, and having a watery good time.

The *Mad Hatter's Tea Party* is a big and small adventure. Children cuddle up to read within the giant teacup. Inside the matching teapot, a mirror ball twirls, motion detectors set off songs, and a fiber-optic spray of tea erupts. A large spoon creates an upholstered seat and the big slice of cake creates a nook for wood block play. The adjacent *March Hare's House,* with its giant ears, has an attic full of costumes, a life-sized table and chairs for dining, and a play kitchen. Other activity stations include the *Reading Forest*, planted with tall flowers and big bugs, the *Cheshire Cat Loft,* filled with books, and the lush *Alice's Garden*, a gated zone perfect for infants and toddlers. All of the sensorial experiences have been designed to help support cognitive learning and the basics of reading. There are many places for children to make art, tell stories, and use their bodies to feel like they are on a journey of major proportions.

1 *Renderings of overall exhibit*   **2** *Early concept elevations*   **3** *Detail renderings of Alice's Pool of Tears*   **4** *Plan layout*

3

2

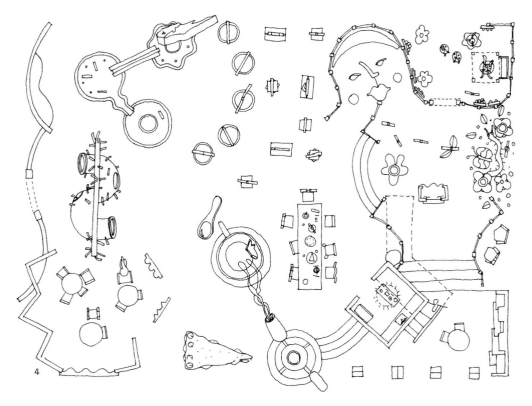

4

InfoTiger's Musical Treasure Hunt
Prototypical exhibit

4

Infotiger's Musical Treasure Hunt is designed as an interactive traveling exhibit that brings Korea's artistic and musical traditions and trends to a young audience. Children come to understand how music transcends cultural boundaries via three-dimensional vignettes, scenes based on Korea's folklore and heritage, as well as its contemporary lifestyle. The environment is filled with natural, traditional materials used both in contrast to and in harmony with synthetic, modern ones. These changes in color, material, and sound help children sense the shifts from traditional to modern and back again.

Glowing paw prints lead to a beast, called InfoTiger, who resides within the entry. Serving as the welcoming committee, he is a veritable treasure chest of Korean information. His embellished chest is a relief map and his soundbites help children locate themselves geographically. InfoTiger is the embodiment of Korean tradition; his form often appears in folk paintings as a model of selflessness, a tiger of wit and wisdom. InfoTiger informs visitors that

1

2

3

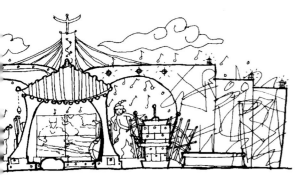

5

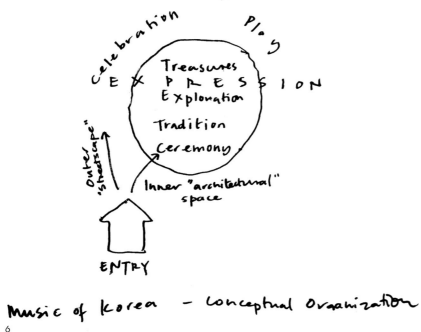

Music of Korea — Conceptual Organization

6

two children, appearing as cutouts with soundbites, have mislaid their personal belongings. Visitors receive a barcoded pass from the tiger, which will play music as they find each consecutive treasure.

Ceremony Court is the first place children venture on their hunt to collect the missing belongings and accumulate musical knowledge. This zone is identified by its iconographic and historical elements. *The Lotus Lounge* is a book nook, *Expressions* is a parade of masks, *Tanch'ong Pavilion* is an architectural kiosk housing a video screen, and the *Circle Stage* is an arena for performing arts. Two bridges lead to another activity zone, *Celebration Court*. Symbolically bridging old and new, these walkways connect to a traditional birthday party and a modern musical marketplace where visitors dance to a simulated dance machine. When all treasures are found, visitors find themselves within the children's bedroom. When the pass is inserted one last time, a sweet farewell song played by the two children is heard. Visitors, young (yin) and old (yang), will be swept up in the emotion and experience conveyed by this exhibit.

Exploratory

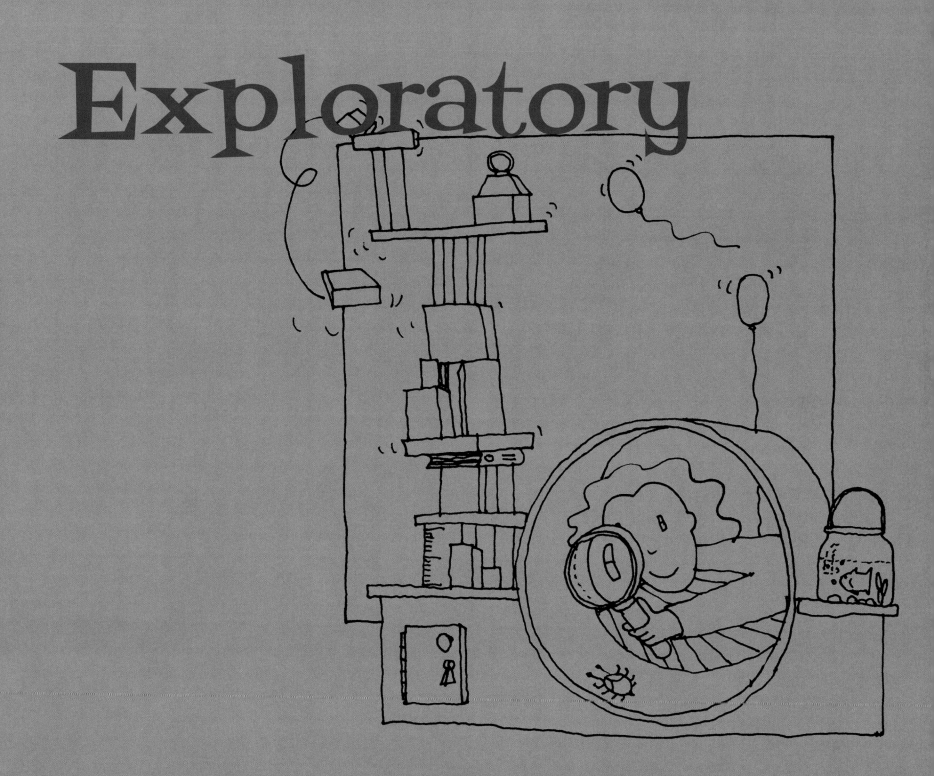

Go Green!

Young At Art Children's Museum Davie, Florida

At the Young At Art Children's Museum, children *Go Green!* A traffic light illuminates this avenue of ecological learning where young visitors explore their environmental consciousness. The familiar and reassuring house façade instills concepts of recycling at home. Interactive learning stations within the home demonstrate how to buy "green" and reclaimed products while also teaching about curbside pick-ups for home recycling efforts. Game-like wall-mounted interactives prompt children with questions about wasteful habits that entertain while teaching the 3Rs: repair, reduce, and reuse.

Set within a park, *Go Green!* teaches visitors of all ages that practicing environmental awareness should be part of everyday life, both at home and in public places. Families perch on recycled lumber benches and discover the nearby trash bins that have soundbites, reminding everyone not to litter and to properly recycle their waste. In this park, trees attract young visitors. Green and magnetic, these leafy branches become the perfect stems

1

RECYCLE HOUSE
WHAT DO THE ITEMS
IN THE WINDOW HAVE IN
COMMON.
STEP INSIDE THE RECYCLE
HOUSE AND FIND OUT.

IT'S RECYCLE DAY

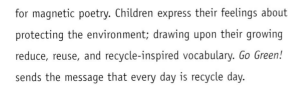

Broward County Recycles

IT'S RECYCLE DAY

Broward County Recycles

2

for magnetic poetry. Children express their feelings about protecting the environment; drawing upon their growing reduce, reuse, and recycle-inspired vocabulary. *Go Green!* sends the message that every day is recycle day.

1 *Children play the recycling game that's fun and good for the environment* **2** *The familiar house façade encourages environmental concern*

Carlson Inquiry Center

Rochester Museum & Science Center Rochester, New York

*T*he *Carlson Inquiry Center*, named for the inventor of the Xerox machine, is a place where scientific inquiry unfolds. The catalyst for Chester Carlson's moment of inspiration was his frustration with copying patents by hand. His place of inquiry was his own kitchen. This center, like Carlson's impromptu lab, is the perfect environment for "blue sky" moments. It is a room full of possibilities: a kitchen, a classroom, a garden, and an open-ended place of scientific enterprise. Its flexible furnishings and adaptable layouts are designed for multiple-age users, for visiting school groups, and for teachers-in-training.

Brainstorming sessions with scientists and staff inspired the open-ended design, which turned a tired demonstration kitchen into a brightly colored place of curiosity. The sky-colored ceiling is filled with magnetic clouds covered in motivational quotes and a trellis that supports electrical equipment for easy access to glue guns, hair dryers, assorted apparatus, and curiosities. The modular carts plug directly into the forest of metal floor posts. These

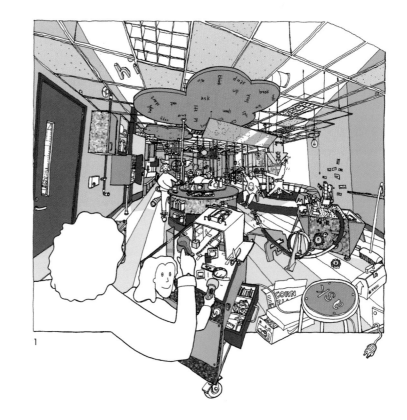

1

1 *Exhibit rendering of scientific possibilities*   **2,3** *Inquiry-based module concepts*

freewheeling carts, called *Intelligence Quests* (IQs), were designed to encourage explorations about nature, wind, water, electricity, air, and sound. *IQ1*, for example, contains air-moving devices, such as fans. The winged, tall cart allows students to send things flying off its fold-down flight deck. By increasing the air pressure on the built-in compressor, students research aeronautics in hands-on ways, from controlling and reading the gauges to taking notes on the dry-erase wings. Ten different incarnations of carts enable students to anticipate, explore, wonder, observe, test, collect, construct, and then inquire, again and again. For those needing a break or wanting to stand on their heads to think, like Carlson often did, a red padded circle in the corner beckons. The red circle reappears throughout the space as a series of buttons, controlling light shows with accompanying soundbites. Students of all ages find that every imaginative visit to the Inquiry Center is an open road to discovery.

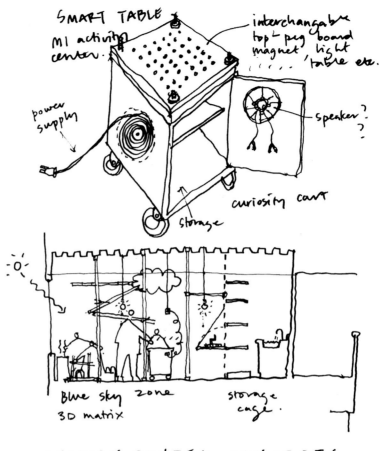

INQUIRY CENTER CONCEPTS

3

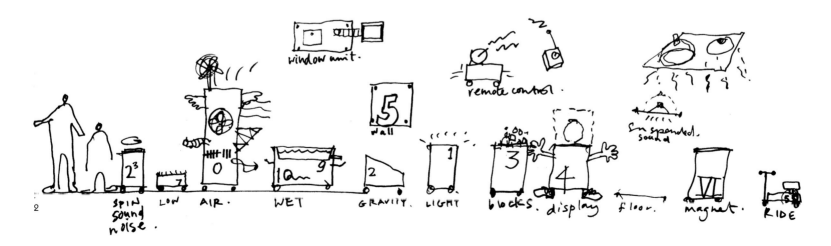

2

Engineering Kids
DuPage Children's Museum Naperville, Illinois

124

The *Engineering Kids* exhibit neighborhood is designed to provide room for children to build their own experiences. These hands-on exhibit zones encourage visitors of all ages to use real tools safely and successfully, helping children develop gross and fine motor skills and eye–hand coordination. By working with real materials and construction equipment, *Engineering Kids* instills a sense of responsibility and privilege. Children become architect, inventor, scientist, and engineer in this innovative exhibit where the focus is on building your own knowledge.

At *Build It*, the construction house, children are thrilled to use the grown-up tools. They learn to respect the use of real nails, hammers, and saws, donning safety goggles and following the rules of behavior. The interior of the construction house is purposely left under construction to further a child's understanding and exploration of building materials. A loft-like space allows children to finish off the roofing, to be up in the ductwork, and to experience a different viewpoint. Attached ↰

1

4 *Collaboratively joining modular components to build and extend the environment around the construction house*   **5** *Modifying simple machines*   **6** *The Make-It-Move environment of kid-controlled machines, ramps, and rollers*

5

4

to the construction house are large pipes, PVC tubes with connectors that children use to build. Creating their structural dreams, kids shape forts, tents, and mazes to run through.

Adjacent to the construction house, *Make-It-Move* features a *Kidnetic Motion Machine* and *Ramps and Rollers*. Both of these components explore forces and motions, encouraging children to build on physics concepts and theories. Creating multiple pathways, children watch the balls roll, jump, swerve, and drop. They watch them travel up and down ramps, through tunnels and around objects, marveling at the energy of motion.

Philosophically, this museum environment promotes an "I can do it" attitude; its open-ended design encourages touch, experimentation, and construction. Kids, in return, learn to respect their environment, equipment, and each other while they build their own worlds.

Wind and Water

Dupage Children's Museum Naperville, Illinois

AirWorks and *WaterWays* present hands-on ways to discover the power, force, and beauty of wind and water. Exhibit areas are designed without signage; families intuitively explore and experiment with flow—this self-control turns visits into powerful experiences.

In the 6-foot-diameter (1.8-meter) transparent tunnel, wind becomes a tangible force in a child's life. Outside the tunnel, everyone can watch as children experiment within the chamber. The wind tunnel has amazing currents of air blowing; children test its force by throwing Frisbees or flying streamers. Wearing a superhero cape over their shoulders, kids feel as strong as the gusting wind. At *Awesome AirWays*, a corresponding wall-mounted interactive, children propel foam balls and scarves into the transparent tubes to watch them being sucked through the air system. The built-in compressor makes the air flow, but children control a series of valves that enable them to change the object's path at junction points. ⇪

2

1 *Masterplan concept rendering of wind and water gallery* **2** *Overall view showing the wind tunnel with Sink and Float Water Table* **3** *Water table detail*

3

6

4

5

At the *Sink and Float Water Table*, children learn how to harness water's power as they play with waterwheels and push tugboats along its streams. Children experience a dry and unique perspective of an underwater world when popping up underneath the acrylic domes. Long and wavy, the table provides ample room for a crowd and allows everyone to find their place at its edge. Its height varies in locations, providing an appropriate space for even the smallest of visitors to watch objects float or sink. When the *Fast Flow Water Table's* overhead tank fills with water, children discharge it, creating a fast, flowing river. The table is sharply angled so water surges down. Children control the water's path, building dams in hope of flooding the premises. It is designed to never overflow, but children have fun trying.

Bubbles is a perennial exhibit favorite and typically a maintenance worry. To keep the bubbles where they belong, the exhibit is partially encircled by huge car wash brushes. Like enormous totems, the brushes delineate the zone. Children also love to wipe their hands on them and squeeze their bodies in-between two brushes, some of which were planned deliberately too close to each other. The concrete flooring was chosen for its durability and the mats for their maintenance ease.

4,5 *Exploring wind forces in the tunnel*
6 *Water table concept sketch*
7 *From the exterior, exhibits are on display; from the inside, children feel like they are playing outside*

7

8 *Prototyping the wind tunnel as part of the design process*   **9** *Popping up underneath the water table*   **10** *Trying to flood the museum at the fast flow water table*   **11** *Discover the science and beauty of bubblemaking*   **12** *Family waterplay*

8

9

10

11

12

Get FIT!

Louisville Science Center Louisville, Kentucky

Growing health and weight concerns led to the development of this traveling exhibit, which delivers the "Get Fit" message in fun and challenging ways. Geared for 8- to 14-year-olds who average four hours a day in front of TVs, computers, and video games, *Get FIT!* gets hearts pounding and bodies moving.

The "core box," a series of climb-on interactive activities, explores the notion of who is fit at work. Using everyday heroes, the exhibit celebrates the health and energy of real people: a chef, a firefighter, a ballet dancer, a construction worker, and a bike messenger. Kids try out occupations, engaging in specific activities that require strength, agility, and endurance. Children see if they have the "heart" to be a firefighter with the cardiovascular ability to climb at the rate of 60 steps a minute while carrying and wearing 75 pounds (34 kilograms) of gear and equipment. *Get FIT!* encourages children to challenge their bodies and minds: beating the clock when climbing the stairs while unwinding the hose as fast and far as ↳

1

3

2

4

5

1 *Kids work out*　**2** *Kids can see if they have the "heart" of a firefighter by running while unwinding the hose*　**3** *A Fit Box module with everyday hero*　**4** *Move pots around, up, and down—it's quite a stretch!*　**5** *Lifting sandbags is a test of your muscular strength; kids can see if they are as fit as construction workers*

possible. Visitors discover that chefs are fit too, as they stretch to reach the pots and stack the dishes. Within the fitness experience, children test their strength and flexibility in ordinary ways that they can easily replicate at home.

The graphic, appealing experiences of *Get FIT!* capture the attention of children and help reintroduce physical play and well-being. Surrounding the core box are colorful shipping crates. Opening them, children discover modular interactives that rethink physical activity, from running obstacle courses to yoga sessions. Visitors of all ages find the dance simulation game module irresistible; its lights and pulsating music have everyone dancing up a storm. Children have so much fun exploring *Get FIT!* they forget that they are working out!

6 *Station to compare your muscular strength with a real-life construction worker* **Opposite** *Kids challenge their firefighting capabilities, testing their desire, endurance, and cardiovascular ability*

Colorforms: It's Time to Play!™

Colorforms®, fondly remembered by parents, continues to offer opportunities for fun, safe, creative, and imaginative play for children from three to eight years of age. Climb right through the exhibit entry, resembling the classic toy box, and a diverse range of art and science activities awaits. This walled entry, reminiscent of the basic set adorned with gold lettering, also houses classic cutout geometric forms with which to experiment. Grab some large, soft-sculpted 3-D shapes (triangle, circle, and line) and stuff the holes within the wall. Look inside the woodblock and find more familiar shapes, which can be applied directly to the wall in decorative or rhythmic forms. On the backside of the famous black box, a display informs visitors of all ages of the nostalgic and historic aspects of this 50-year-old toy.

Many times in history a bathroom or a kitchen becomes a zone of serendipitous invention. In the *Bathroom of Invention*, visitors learn how two artists first invented the toy. Given a supply of self-adhesive vinyl to play

with, the couple soon discovered that the cut shapes stuck easily to their bathroom walls. It was so much fun to play with, the couple created the Colorforms® product line. Within the exhibit bathroom, children and caregivers experiment firsthand with this toy that has "stuck" around for 50 years. The real bathtub with its translucent "water" surface (backlit with changing LED lights) creates a horizontal plane used for patternmaking. The shiny floor is also a place for experimenting and creating patterns. Within the kitchen, discoveries are made when playing with vacuums, suction, and magnets. In this familiar place, children and caregivers use suction cups, plungers, and robotic wall-walkers to better understand the force of suction as well as the related properties of magnetic attraction.

Another opportunity for self-expression is the Archi-Forms —a backdrop of architectural landmarks where young architects draft their own designs, adding them to the city landscape. Additionally, story-telling tablets with magnetic panels and easels provide a limitless canvas for visitors' artistic imagination, drafting skills, or poetic expression.

Colorforms is a registered trademark of University Games.

1–4 *Concept sketches*

Public

The Pritzker Family Children's Zoo
Lincoln Park Zoo Chicago, Illinois

142

1 *Looking at nature*   **2** *The clearing in the woods*   **3** *The entry pylon*

As one of Chicagoland's exemplary childhood destinations, the Pritzker Family Children's Zoo embodies a commitment to providing valuable naturalistic experiences for families. The design is a collaboration of learning environment and landscape and a synthesis of indoors and out-of-doors. The resulting destination is fun to explore and a great childhood place to return to, again and again.

Engaging adult and child, the renovated children's zoo shifts the paradigm of typical hands-on zoo learning through the construction of relevant experience. The unique integration of the man-made interior woods, the landscape and animal habitats, and the multi-generational experiences creates an extraordinary, safe, and accessible walk in the woods for visitors of all ages and learning styles.

Among visual and structural tree trunks, the canopy climber soars 20 feet (6 meters) into the air indoors. Constructed of curved pieces of poplar plywood that

1

2

3

children climb or crawl on, the canopy is a full mind and body experience. Webs of silver cable safely nestle children as they ascend to new heights and discover the best views of the patterned terrariums and aviary. Below, viewing windows and touch tanks permit closer viewing of animals while related activities like the beaver water table connect a hands-on experience with the reality. The interior conveys the impression of the woods in springtime, enhanced by natural illumination and the view to the outside.

Outdoors along the walk, the interpretive pylons and the clearing in the woods are beautifully crafted educational devices. Made of steel twigs and sticks, the bronzed clearing canopy opens up into an arena perfect for programs,

4

5

performances, or rest. The pylons inform visitors about the animals and their habitats in multiple ways. Each habitat has a corresponding hands-on interactive—observe and then experience. For example, the smell box encourages you to learn about a bear's heightened senses by using your own.

The children's zoo is composed of layers of exhibits and matching experiences that foster affinities between children and woodland creatures. Through art, architecture, and habitat, children come to appreciate the need for husbandry of the environment and gain a better understanding of the animals sharing our locale and our ecosystem. The Pritzker Family Children's Zoo is designed as a beautiful home in the woods.

8

4 *The walk in the woods in the context of the city*
5 *The clearing is a gathering place surrounded by the woods*
6,7 *The clearing's tunnels provide opportunities to rest, view, and roam* 8 *Like toys in the landscape, animal pylons interpret corresponding habitats*

6

7

9,10,12 *Engaging in animal-like behavior: looking, touching, and smelling as if you were a bear* **11** *Bear pylon design sketch*
13 *Building like a beaver*

9

10

16

17

18

14,15 *Interpretive, interactive signage interests and informs visitors*   **16,17** *Make sounds and listen as if you were an otter*

18 *Howl like a wolf*

Opposite *The interior mimics the colors, patterns, textures, rhythm, and density of the adjacent woodland walk* **20,21** *Crawl and climb through the treetop canopy climber* **22,23** *The canopy climber surrounds the soft-sculpture storytelling stump like a theater*

22

23

24 *Dappled sunlight shines through the woodland canopy* **25** *The canopy shades the terrariums and their animals* **26** *The docent and visitor "look closer"* **27** *Children see woodland habitats alongside a snake*

25

24

26

27

28

29

28 *Beaver water table*   **29** *Turtle tank alongside the beaver viewing window*   **30** *Damming the stream as if you were a beaver*   **31** *Seeing the beauty of nature in the woods*

30

31

South Pond Nature Center

Lincoln Park Chicago, Illinois

For more than 140 years, the South Pond at Lincoln Park has served as an urban retreat and a wildlife refuge, but it is now showing its age. The enhancement project will enable the pond to become self-sustaining, repair its perimeter edge, and increase the opportunities for visitors to interact. The pond will become a welcome respite and natural amenity for zoo visitors strolling along its banks. Lovely, iconographic swan boats will be added to the fleet of paddleboats so passengers can take peaceful cruises around the lagoon and see the new habitat up close.

The South Pond will also become an outdoor nature center, permitting school groups to engage in scientific enterprise. Children and teachers will work from the new jetty that extends right into the pond, allowing hands-on exploration of the elements of its ecosystem: birds, insects, fish, mammals, and the force of water that sustains them all. Outdoor leaning nodes help children foster an affinity for the natural world and develop an instinct to conserve it. Children and teachers will conduct wildlife research in

1

their own urban environment, their own "backyard." Curiosity carts and interactive learning pylons line the newly constructed edge. All visitors, from young scientists to avid zoo visitors, will benefit from the South Pond's enhancements and educational interpretation. Reinterpreting this lovely area as a nature center encourages visitors of all ages and interests to be more aware of the foliage and wildlife that make their home within Lincoln Park's South Pond.

1,2 *Concept illustrations of self-guided family activities by the pond*

2

4

3,4 *Concept illustrations of families or school groups engaging in facilitated activities*

Evanston Public Library Children's Library and Teen Center

Evanston, Illinois

The educationally informed design of the *Children's Library and Reading Gardens* takes its imagery from art and stories, secret gardens, and an ever-changing landscape that is irresistible to children. The *KinderSpring* light fountain welcomes visitors and helps create a sense of place. Children and caregivers gather around its inviting mosaic form, covered in tiles and words with an iridescent fiber-optic flow.

Within the formal setting of the main library, literary-based environments for spontaneous, informal, and programmed interaction were developed for children to explore the world of reading. *Mac's Garden*, a quiet and sheltered garden, is perfect for infant and toddler exploration. Toddlers enjoy the buzz of activity at the *Garden Gates*, where preschoolers plant alphabet flowers and test keys that open *Discovery Boxes*. School-age children find their place in the *Art Gardens* with their troughs full of raw constructive materials, reminiscent of the Johnson Wax building's revered desks.

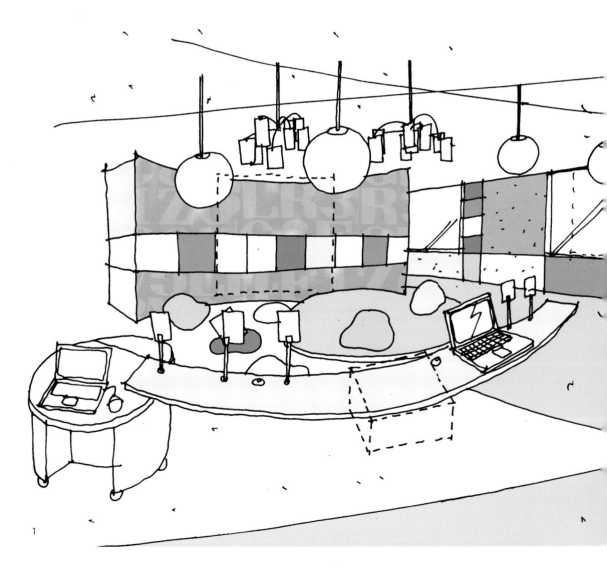

1

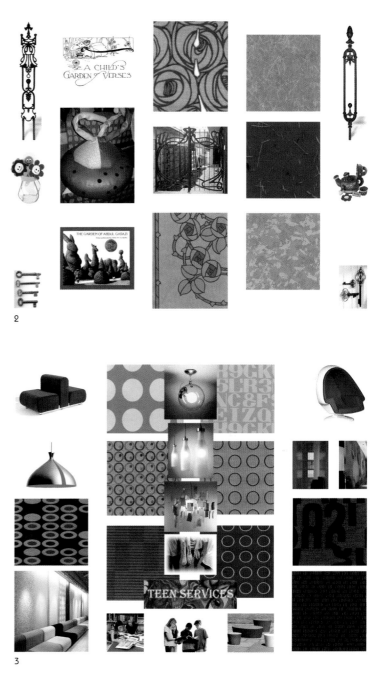

2

3

1 Concept rendering of teen center **2,3** Palette of materials, finishes, and furniture

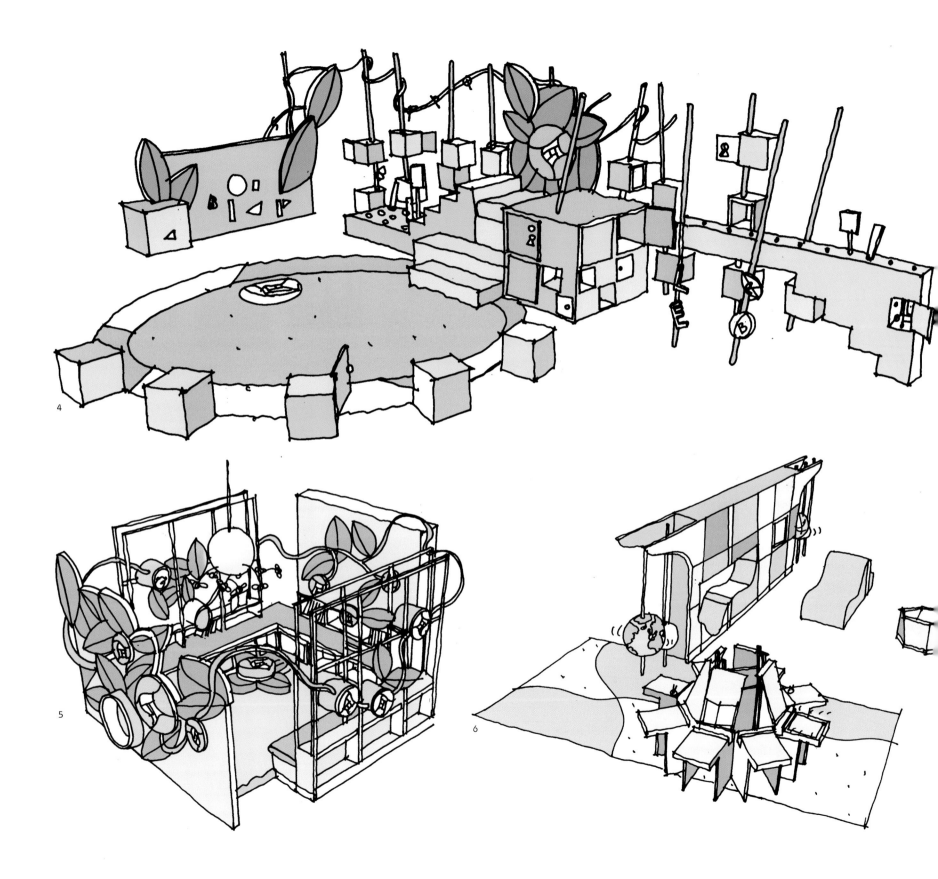

In harmony with the library's Prairie-based architectural style, the design of the children's library takes inspiration from Frank Lloyd Wright with its craftsman aesthetics. Tucked inside the entry, the *Garden Gazebo* encourages families to read together; this structure consists of kid-friendly columns with insets of stained glass, peek-a-boo pickets, and movable puppet theatre. Octagami™, an eight-sided art and game station, holds literary illustrations and the Hexagami™ stools double as seating and curiosity cabinets. The scale of the elements, millwork, and furnishings shifts from low and petite to giant and oversized. Children relish these fluctuating aspects that create accessibility, intrigue, and visibility. The interior's carefully constructed landscape with its meandering paths and centers for play, art, story, and performance encourage children to make their own choices.

Brainstorming with the young adult advisory panel, a *Teen Scene* was created that is separate, but not isolated from the main library. Preferring the prairie sensibilities to current trends, teens advocated for flexibility with accessibility to staff and reference materials. A palette expressive of their ideas represented a duality: a "silly" side with egg chairs, mood lights, and space to lounge and a "serious" side with study carrels and task lighting. Bringing everything together is the *Reading Bar*, a café-inspired long counter surrounding a stage for performance.

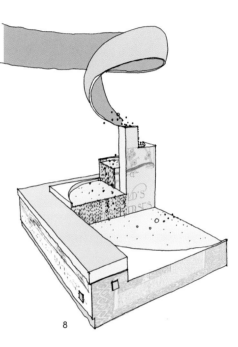

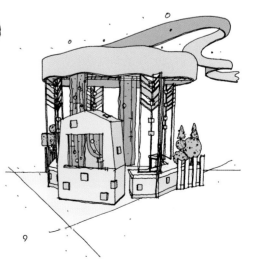

4 *Garden Gates storytelling and discovery area for toddlers*   **5** *Mac's Garden zone for caregivers and infants*   **6** *Hexagami, Octagami, and the young readers' media wall*   **7** *Art garden*   **8** *KinderSpring, a fountain of lights, illuminating and animating the entry*   **9** *The Garden Gazebo*

Kids on the Fly

O'Hare International Airport Chicago, Illinois

1 Flying out of the cargo chute   2 Celebrating air travel   3 Kids on the Fly as destination   4 Final exhibit renderings   5 In the accessible cargo plane cockpit   6 Inside interactive cargo crate

The *Kids on the Fly* exhibit is designed to celebrate air travel, presenting young travelers with a hands-on playful introduction to aviation. Beyond its appeal as a welcome relief from airport delays and stopovers, the satellite exhibit is envisioned as a cultural amenity that enhances and encourages use of the world's busiest airport. The program calls for a dynamic, safe, and secure environment to replicate the quality and mission of the main children's museum, setting a new standard for stand-alone exhibits.

Located within a very active terminal, the exhibit is sited to make visitors feel as if they are on the runway itself. A variety of multi-sensory experiences were created, from loading freight to monitoring the real goings-on at O'Hare via electronic elements in the simulated control tower. An interactive activity center was developed in collaboration with aviation staff. Under the shadow of a giant Lego™ Sears Tower, children rebuild and plan Chicago's downtown using constructive blocks.

1

2

3

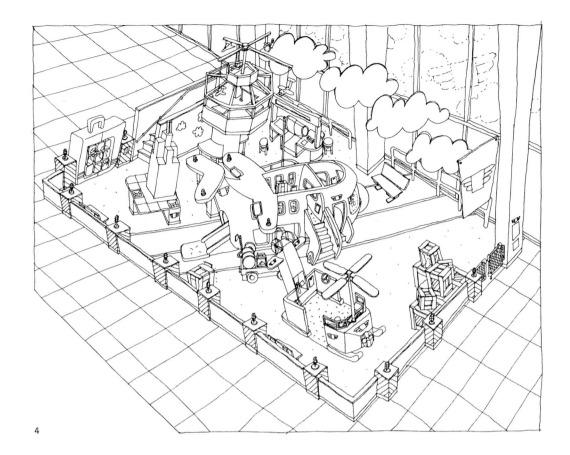

4

Focusing on universal appeal and accessibility as important design criteria, this environment allows visitors of all ages and abilities the freedom to control their experiences. At *Kids on the Fly*, the most interesting way to enter the cargo plane is via the colorful, activity-filled incline. Instead of treating the ramp in a subordinate architectural manner, it is celebrated as the primary entry and as a source of play. Children enter the raised cockpit, pilot the plane, listen to recordings of air traffic control, and have a great view of real take-offs and landings.

The design responds to the qualitative standards expected by a premier cultural institution and through thoughtful coordination and detailing, deals with the extraordinary traffic and maintenance requirements inherent to an international airport. The *Kids on the Fly* satellite exhibit was awarded an American Institute of Architects Interior Architecture Award for its unique design and accessibility.

5

6

8

Children's Midway, Garden in a City
Chicago, Illinois

Garden in a City is America's first garden and landscape design show focusing on urban horticulture. The inaugural season of this in-ground show features an interactive Children's Midway where children and families will find engaging and educational interactives that relate to the greening of our urban community. The mayor's mission is that Garden in a City be another demonstration of the city's commitment to preserve and protect the natural environment. Working toward a goal of making Chicago the most environmentally friendly city in America, the Children's Midway provides a pathway of green, hands-on, fun experiences.

Giant cutout flowers and enormous plant pots grace the trellis entry. Children crawl though the flower tunnels and mini-slides to find a garden of fun and activity. The design of the midway accentuates scale and uses ordinary gardening equipment in surprising, fun ways. At the Big Soil Play Area, kids dig and get dirty at large, industrial troughs of sod and rocks. They plant their own take-home

1

1 *Garden in a City: the Children's Midway at the annual garden show*   **2,5** *Concept sketches*   **3** *Banner graphic*   **4** *Floral tunnel of fun*

2

5

3

4

seedlings and learn how to care for them. The nearby trellis supports a musical maze of hoses and sprinklers. There are wet and dry routes; young visitors find paths of their own choosing. Oversized, "smelly" pots line the walk, designed as planters of fragrant flowers and intriguing shapes to sniff and wonder about. Visitors of all ages learn to distinguish the scent of lavender, mint, lilacs, grass, and even manure.

At the *Butterfly Tent*, children make the paper caterpillars, butterflies, and bugs that adorn its canopy. It is a center for creative activity. The city's park district supplies programming, which includes painting rocks, rubbing bark, and designing seed packets. There is also a daily parade of children, parents, and red wagons filled with plants that marches along the gardens. ✒

6

The *Children's Midway* creates a similar learning experience to that which adult visitors have at *Garden in a City*. In this space, children will learn how the greening of our spaces improves our communities and the quality of our lives by engaging in gardening first hand.

7

6,7 *Concept sketches*   **8,opposite** *Playing in the garden under the hose pipe and watering can trellis*   **10** *Picnic table program activity*

8

10

Cultural

Children's Museum of Brownsville

Brownsville, Texas

The Children's Museum of Brownsville is its own border town, a destination for learning, playfully bringing together Mexican and American culture, history, and lore. Its design reflects the sunshine and beauty of its Resaca environs, while responding to critical education and health issues arising from its active and porous border along the Rio Grande.

El Primero Mercado, the marketplace, is the heart of the museum, celebrating the local spirit of buying and selling with its regional look and use of indigenous materials. Children creatively use the movable *Vendadores*, traveling carts, for face-painting and staging puppet shows. The traditional fountain is lush and lyrical, with local artifacts, mosaic, and scrabble tiles lining its tiered shape. It reminds young visitors of how precious water is in this region, using fiber optics to produce its radiant flow. Marking the marketplace perimeter are "bell trees", metal cutouts planted in and outdoors, which hold captivating chimes and *mache de papel* birds. The palette derives from

THE CHILDREN'S MUSEUM OF
BROWNSVILLE
BROWNSVILLE, TX

1 *View from the entry lobby*　**2** *Rendering of final design*　**3** *Rendering of animated entry*

regional color, inspired by the river and the earth. Materials and finishes cross borders too; the sensorial Tac-Tiles that run along the museum walls include squares of pressed tin, tooled leather, hand-painted birdhouses, and handcrafted tiles.

All around the museum are opportunities to role-play in themed zones, from the family farm to the folk-tale inspired *Sea Serpent Infant Zone*. The medical role-play zone promotes healthy practices. Children become doctors and nurses, brushing oversized teeth, taking temperatures, and giving immunizations. The *All-Worlds Restaurant* teaches children about diverse diets and nutrition with its farm-grown Texas oranges and valley grapefruits. At the adjacent farm, children plant and pick ripe fruit, loading the pickup truck for daily restaurant delivery. Concepts for the core exhibits stem from collaborative design with children and the community. *Dance With Me* highlights multicultural dances and the *Little Isabella Lighthouse* is modeled after the local beacon, but patterned with tiles of visitors' handprints. As an educational frontier, the design of the children's museum blends the diversity of its bicultural community with educational messages through play and with pride.

The Children's Museum
of Brownsville

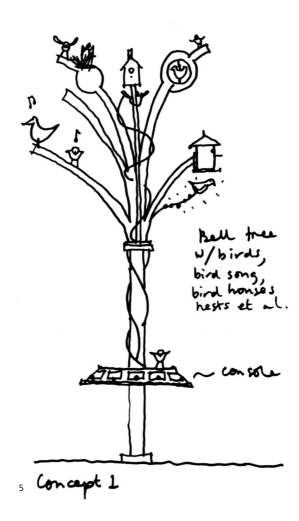

Bell tree
w/birds,
bird song,
bird houses
nests et al.

~ console

Concept 1

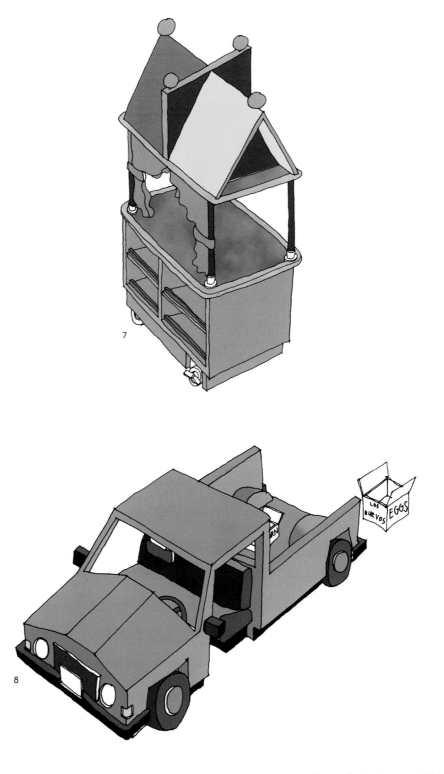

4 *Museum logo*   **5** *Design sketch of bell tree*   **6** *View of marketplace and Resaca*   **7** *Vendadore design sketch*   **8** *Pickup truck design sketch*

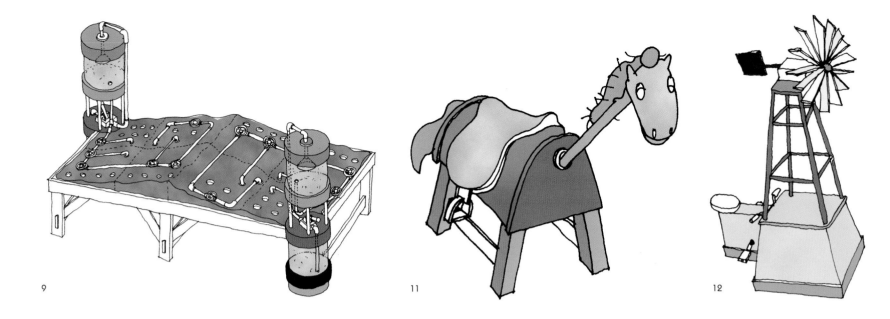

9

11

12

10

13

14

16

15

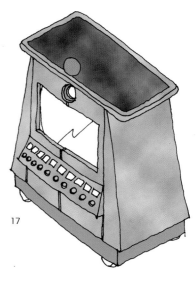

17

9,11,12 *Farm and weather interactive design sketches*   **10,13** *All-World's restaurant*   **14** *Multipurpose room*   **15** *Shrimp boat design sketch*   **16** *Dance With Me performance space*   **17** *Dance With Me interactive video cabinet design sketch*

19

20

21

22

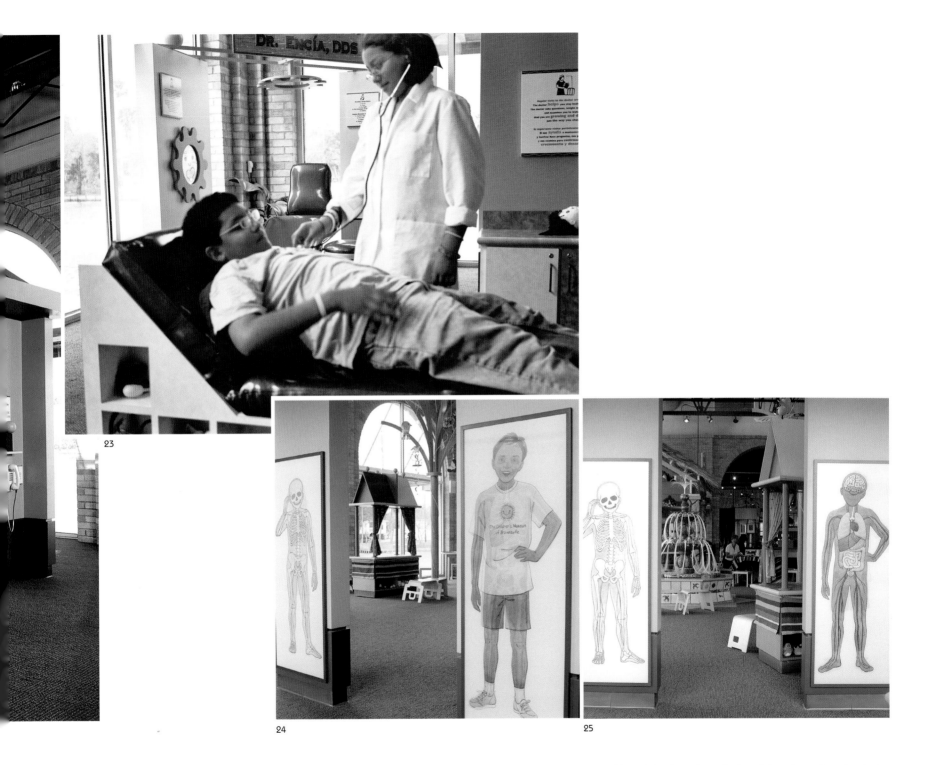

23

24

25

21–25 *Encouraging healthy habits through medical and dental practice role-playing*

26

27

26 *Overall museum view*   **27** *The farmhouse*   **28** *The weather play area framed by the Little Isabella Lighthouse and sailboat*   **29** *The Sea Serpent infant zone*

28

29

Alliance Française Chez Kids Academy
Chicago, Illinois

The entry to the *Chez Kids Academy* is through a welcoming series of graphic French and English messages. Children immediately understand that this bright and spirited space has been designed just for them. In *La Classe,* activity centers encourage the spoken and written word. Discovery boxes, found nearby at the *Museé D'Objets* wall, are full of multicultural books, puzzles, and games. A brightly colored *castelet*, a traditional puppet theater, resides in *Le Theatre*, and represents a rich tradition of dramatic experience that is difficult for children of all ages to resist. Children gain access to a virtual Francophone gateway via the internet, *Le Café*, and its adjacent library. Well-stocked with books, supplies, maps, atlases, and mini-clocks, from digital to cuckoo, this nook is the perfect place to spend some time, relaxing and reading. The *Celebrations* changing exhibit wall allows teachers and students to pin up work and items of interest, and also use the dry-erase panels for lessons and announcements.

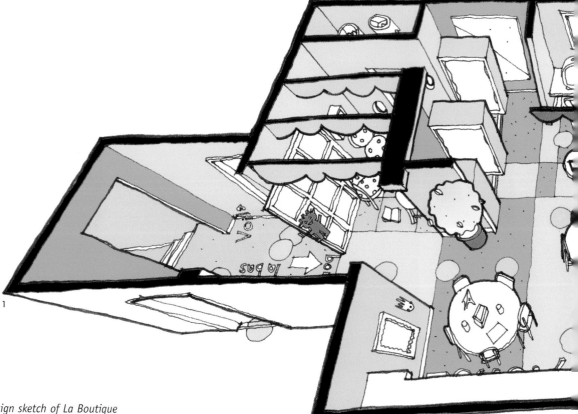

1

1 *Rendering of Chez Kids Academy*   **2** *View of La Boutique*   **3** *Design sketch of La Boutique*

3

2

The children's center is a passport for intercultural learning; it takes young visitors on a language journey all around the globe! This rich and tactile environment is filled with many discoveries of traditional and contemporary French culture, society, and art, all interjected in stimulating, fun-filled zones. The goals of Chez Kids Academy match school standards, exploring and appreciating communication, culture, and geography while forming foundations for understanding.

4 *Design sketches, clockwise from top left: Entry, La Cabane, La Boutique, Le Cybercafé,*
Le Musée et Le Theatre, Le Café

6

Song of Korea

Children's Museum of Austin Traveling Exhibit

*S*ong of Korea, an evocative and engaging exhibit, brings this nation's sounds and rhythms to a wide audience of young visitors. Wandering in and out of the entry, a shadowbox portal of graphics, images, artifacts, and sounds, children discover the welcoming song of Korea.

Cutouts of real Korean children with integrated sound chips stand and speak as ambassadors, inviting visitors to each neighborhood. Working with Korean and American educators, the design team visualized a series of interactive zones that illustrate both ancient traditions and contemporary lifestyle. Incorporating authentic materials, instruments, and sensorial experiences, these neighborhoods encourage children to take part in Korean everyday life. At *Grandfather's Drum Workshop*, children join in a Lunar New Year celebration to learn how tradition is passed from generation to generation. In a simulation of modern urban high-rise living, families visit friends for spicy Korean foods and engage in dinner conversation. Korean culture sustains a strong belief in the power of education

1

1 *Exhibit graphic*   2 *The portal encourages children to look closer at the images, treasures, and sights of Korea*   3 *Ambassadors of sight and sound lead children and their caregivers through the playful environments*

and hard work; visiting an example of an elementary school demonstrates this philosophy. Moving into a *Noraebang*, a Karaoke singing room, children dance and sing along to traditional and K-Pop (Korean pop) songs. Shifting from zone to zone, children role-play, dress up, and become more attuned to this nation's sights and sounds. The rhythm of daily Korean life is explored through play, teaching children about Asian cultures by appealing to their natural curiosity.

Children visiting this cultural playroom actively connect to the Korean experience. Beautiful to see and hear, the *Song of Korea* encourages musical experiences, constructs new cultural understandings, and builds respect for tradition and family through play.

2

3

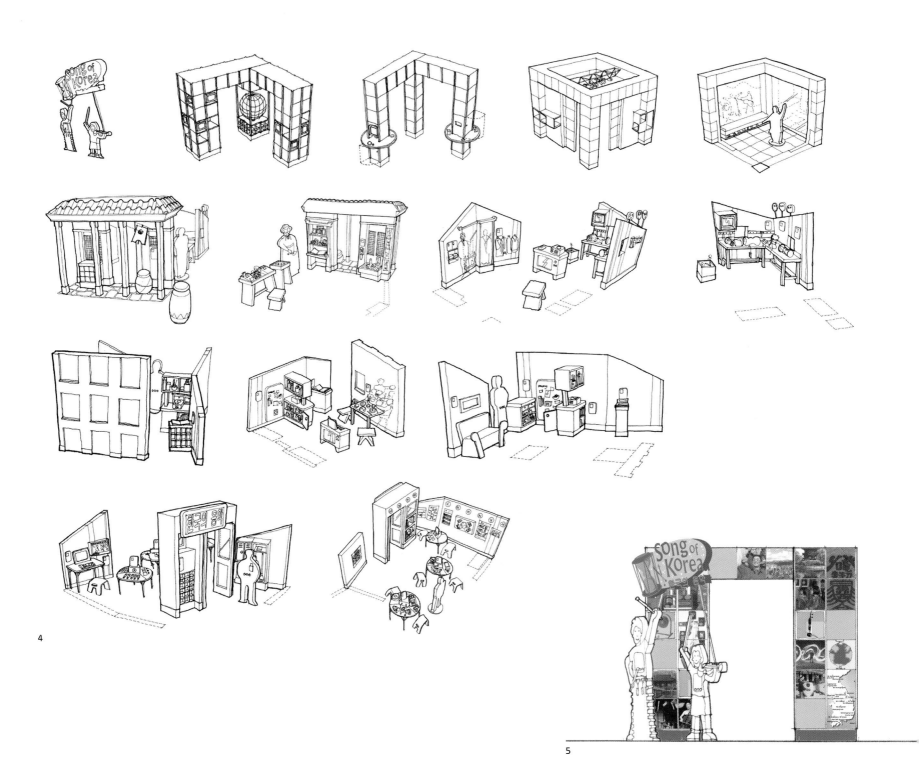

6

7

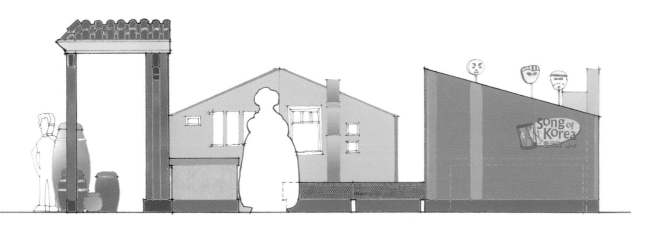

4 *Rendering of exhibit kits of parts*   **5** *Exhibit elevation*   **6** *Visit a rural home with walls of paper that open into the craftsman's workshop*   **7** *Where is Korea?*

8

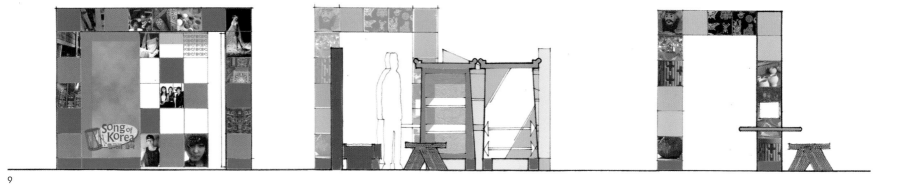

9

10

8–10 *Exhibit elevations*   **11** *Making tea*   **12** *Children sit down for dinner with a welcoming Korean family*

11

12

13 *Face-to-face with Korean artifacts*   **14** *At the Norebang, children sing and dance traditional and modern songs*   **Opposite** *Explore the workshop of a master drummaker*
16 *You can sing and dance to the top ten K-Pop songs*

13

14

16

Nyumba Home Place

Kentucky Center for African American Heritage Louisville, Kentucky

Nyumba is a community of culture, play, and understanding. In many languages spoken in Africa, Nyumba translates as *Home Place*. One enters the children's gallery by traveling through a quilted corridor of unusual textures, images, and shadow boxes filled with treasured historical and cultural artifacts. Within the exhibit, trees are important architectural elements, emblematic of the recurring theme of shelter and space. For children everywhere, trees are consistent, recognizable, and iconic elements. They remind one of creating spaces, as in dens and tree houses, or of climbing, or of the perspective only achieved from being up high. Here, the trees create a rhythmic canopy above the corridor that leads directly to Nyumba.

Visible from the entry is the *Front Porch*, reminiscent of the common familial setting of Kentucky's African American experience. Evoking the mood of a relaxing social occasion, the porch features rockers, games, banjos, and guitars. It opens into *Grandma's Kitchen*,

1

where children discover histories of the everyday and extraordinary members of Kentucky's African American community. Traveling trunks highlight each role model's story through hands-on collections of artifact and story. In the yard, the Celebration Tree, a sculptural rendition of Kentucky's yellow poplar, proudly displays children's artwork in southern folk-art form. Washboards, plastic buckets, and a big bass drum encourage musical activity. The winding recycled rubber street becomes a daily parade path for children to march along as they play their chosen instruments. It also provides proper surfacing for hopscotch, jump rope, and hand-clapping games.

The *Horizons of Africa* presents symbolic elements: a huge stylized *Baobab Tree* and the *Bountiful Spring*. Known as the Tree of Life, the Baobab tree is emblematic of hope, freedom, and heritage. Here, the ancient stylized tree becomes a place of physical challenge and discovery. Children dress up as lions, elephants, and rhinoceroses, climbing on and around the tree, its upturned roots, and the ecosystem it supports. Shaped like the continent of Africa, the *Bountiful Spring* has water flowing down in channels and desert areas filled with sand. Other areas within *Nyumba* include a computer room, an art-making room, and small adaptable work platforms for building and inventing where children can create their own worlds —their own home place.

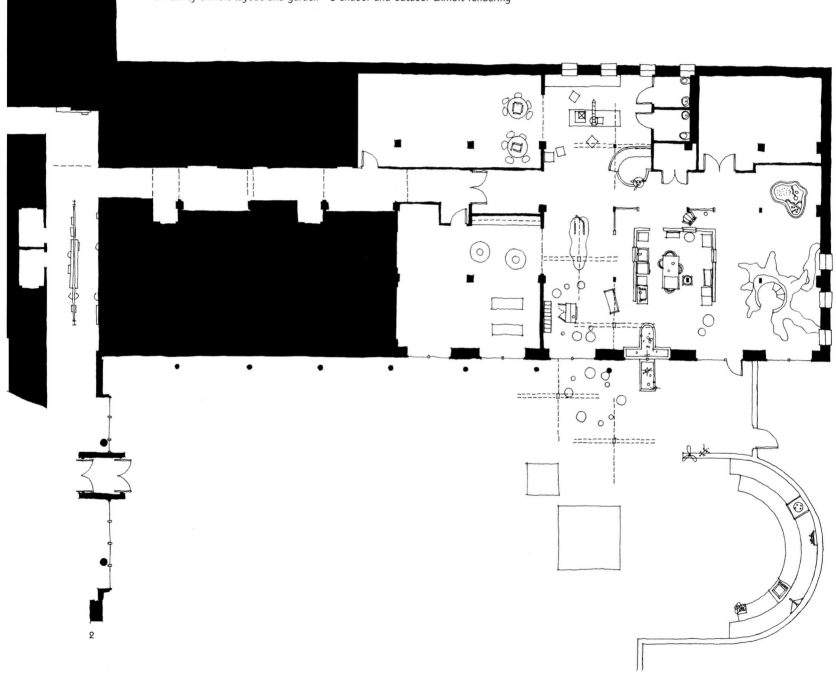

2 *Plan of exhibit layout and garden* **3** *Indoor and outdoor exhibit rendering*

2

3

Spiritual

Granger Community Church Children's Ministry

Granger, Indiana

This children's facility is "mission-driven" in both focus and design, fostering purposeful play by using biblical teachings as its foundation. Community leaders hope that children will use their environments to learn and to positively influence their families. Parents also find the colorful, themed spaces captivating, and are inherently drawn into the experiential world of their child. The sensorial design of the children's ministry turned typical, institutional classrooms into engaging experiences. Children ask to return each and every weekend and to bring their friends, increasing attendance figures by more than 60 percent. The children's ministry, an instant hit with more than 800 children, became so successful that within two years an expansion occurred. The center's 32,000 square feet (3000 square meters) of interactivity now accommodate 1500 children, and offer families innovative experiences to promote spiritual awareness in ways that are culturally relevant. ✒

1 *The Nursery Train That Could environment is the perfect "vehicle" of an infant's comfort, safety, social, and spiritual growth*　**2** *Details of Nursery Train: brightly colored engines and cars have blowing smoke stacks and interactive cabins; some cars double as changing tables with mats, safety straps, and diaper supplies*

3 *Enter this constructive community via a sewer pipe to gear up with tool belts and aprons*

4 *Construction trailer is a theater for religious stories and puppet shows*

7

8

9

Opposite *Inspired by the story of Jonah and the Big Fish, children slide into the Under the Sea zone through the fish's mouth* **6** *Slide entrance and activity playstations* **7** *Intergalactic, inspirational journey awaits children 5 to 7 years old in 3-2-1 Penguins™* **8** *3-2-1 Penguins™, a space-age adventure based on the Big Idea Productions video series, offers a galaxy of play and learning opportunities* **9** *Taking off!*

11

12

13

Iconographic and symbolic elements, which children easily understand, make all feel welcome and safe. Themed environments are designed to be age- and purpose-specific, such as the nursery where infants and toddlers focus on the high contrast, tactile trains and manipulative landscape. Two-year-olds work the farm with an abundance of hands-on activities and three-year-olds tend the farm garden. Preschoolers and school-age children enjoy adventures too, including a seashore of activity, an intergalactic mission of "parable" proportion, and constructive play. Older children earn their wings at *Heir Force*, a runway built for performance and spirituality.

Transforming the ubiquitous dreary Sunday school basement into vibrant, energetic children's spaces, the church practices what it preaches: that faith and form are found in the humblest of places. Hundreds of community leaders have toured this world-class facility, making it a national reference for designing children's church facilities. The Children's Ministry is kid-friendly, stimulating, and transformational: its existence creates a new paradigm for church leaders.

Opposite *Heir Force's older kids earn their wings at this airfield of fun where they practice controlling strength and power* **11** *Heir Force runway, cut into the linoleum, creates a perfect zone for large group congregation while the scaffolding form of a plane flies overhead* **12** *All rooms have formal and informal places for performance and storytelling* **13** *Wide gallery corridors are welcoming and iconic*

14

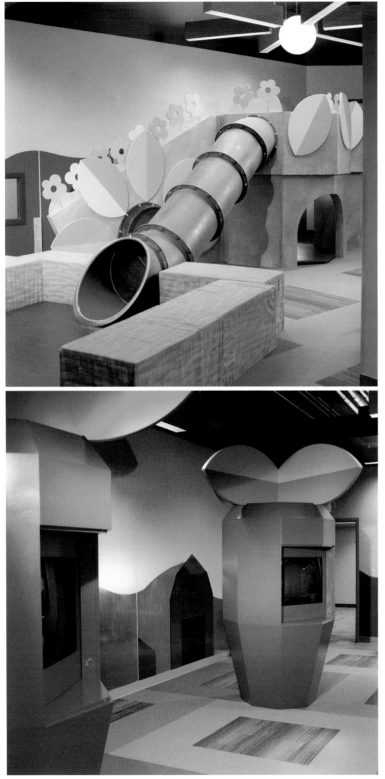

15

17

16

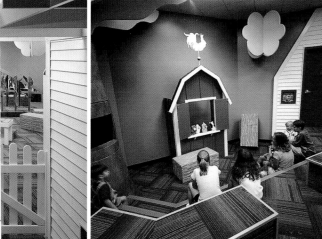

18

19

14 *Farm garden slide for preschoolers*   **15** *Stage area with carrot monitors*   **16** *Familiar farmyard friends are activity tables*   **17** *Two-year-olds cultivate their spiritual awareness in the warm atmosphere of the Working Farm, complete with picket fence and full-size cow plus abundant hands-on activities*   **18** *Barnyard Theater creates opportunities for expressive play*   **19** *The big chicken*

From this calming environment, children are happy for their parents to go on to the service while they follow the clear signage and stepping-stones (islands, clouds, paw prints, and lines) that lead children to their individual classrooms.

Children arrive at their themed classrooms that share modularity and an efficient flexibility of design. Each themed classroom follows a consistent layout with a central stage, an open space, and nooks for art and reading. "Instructional Walls", panels of dry-erase, magnetic, and pin-board surfaces, allow teachers varying methods of communicating current objectives, parables, and examples. "ME-Zones" display and celebrate children's creations using picture rails, shadowboxes, and cork surfaces. Children and adult volunteers work either in large groups for drama or in small groups for discussion, activity, and prayer. Developmentally, emotionally, and spiritually, opportunities have been created at *Crosstown* to present imagery that relates to Biblical stories and which encourages appropriate role-play and exploration.

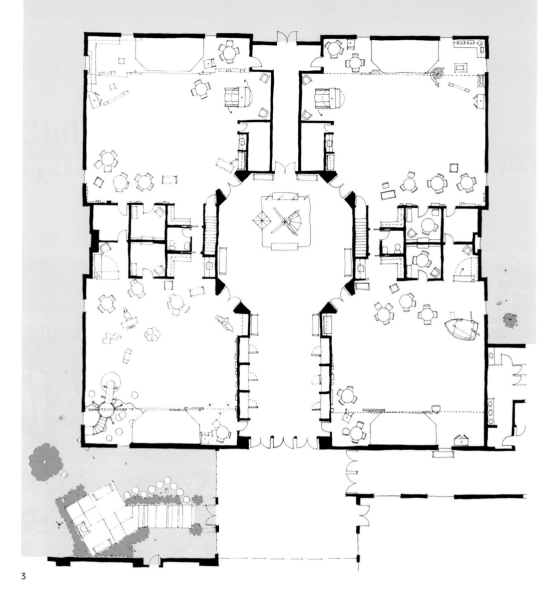

3

4

5

7

3 *Plan layout*   **4** *Classroom elevation*   **5** *Rendering of entry*   **6,8** *Classroom elevations*   **7** *Village Green concept sketch*

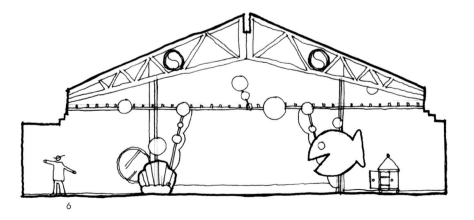

6

8

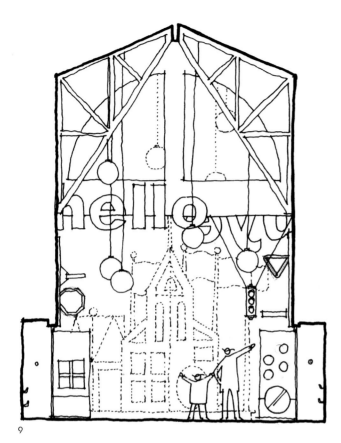

9

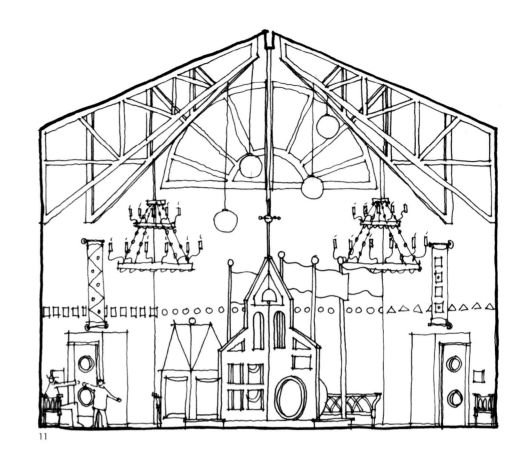

11

10

12

9,11 *Entry and Village Green elevations*
10 *Classroom detail*   **12–14** *Village Green details*

14

13

Promiseland and Adventure Club

Northeast Christian Church Louisville, Kentucky

Northeast Christian Church imaginatively provides children with spiritual spaces; its new ministry focuses on bridging play, sharing, adventure, and caring with Biblical learning. Families gather in the Village Green, a long, indoor green space where children and caregivers orient themselves before heading off to services or their classrooms. Standing in the center of the green is a small pavilion, reminiscent of a traditional church, which provides both a focal point and a meeting center. Doubling as a movable stage and play place with crawl-in tubes, the pavilion creates a zone of quiet activity.

Three-, four-, and five-year-olds find their place in the *Promiseland* classroom. Modularity and flexibility optimize what happens in each room, from performance to prayer. Children and teachers work in large or small groups for music, drama, and teaching. Each room's imagery derives from a continent and its animals, from South America's exotic birds to Asia's pandas. Consistent, yet distinctive layouts increase the efficiency of the design of the

1

1 *Rendering of entry* **2** *Rendering of Adventure Club*

classrooms and their integrated elements. Book nooks and crannies double as alcoves. Carts supply art props and materials. Instructional walls are created from dry erase, magnetic, and pin-board panels. ME-Zone tactile panels become an interactive gallery displaying the children's work.

For older children, the two-story design of the *Adventure Club* has symbolic, humorous, and sophisticated overtones. It is filled with physical and spiritual challenges. Lining *Creation Corridor* are interactive spaces, rooms within the larger, open space. *Holey Walls*, the *Crown Room*, and the *Ark* are symbolic, fun arenas for game-playing, reading, computer interaction, and art-making. The stage features a climbing canopy made of curved wood steps encased in metal mesh. Children safely climb up and through, pausing to overlook performances.

The children's ministry's highly animated spaces encourage diverse experiences, from Biblical play to prayer. Having a dedicated children's center increases the church's potential for reaching out to children and the community in ways they understand.

2

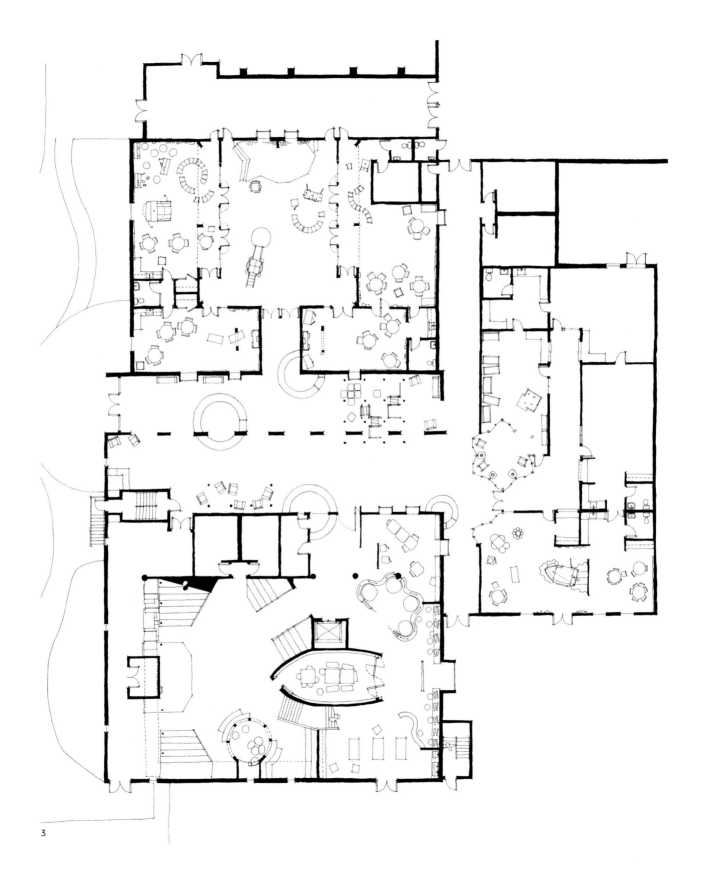

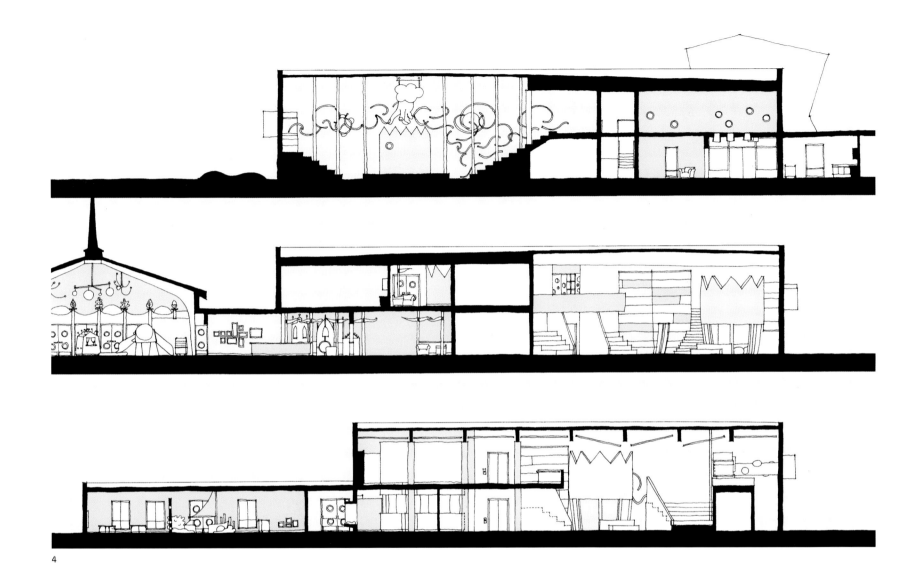

4

3 *Plan layout*   **4** *Elevations*

Turnpoint Apostolic Church Children's Ministry

Groveport, Ohio

In the beginning, there was *Bible Boulevard*. Designed as a family thoroughfare and functioning as a spine, it is the first stop for families entering the children's center. Covered with cheerful graphics and very big words, *In the Beginning* provides dramatic imagery while highlighting scripture. *Prayer and Play Telephones* provide interactive elements; children pick up the phones and listen to snippets of Biblical tales, seasonal messages, and parables. Multiple tracks keep the messages fresh and ever changing.

The Promised Land Play Stage is a variant of a *passion play* and a playground. The numerous façades include a semblance of the stable or tented canopy. A play zone with a climbing wall, formed from brightly colored resin squares with funky footholds, presents a wonderful body and spirit challenge. This is also the performance zone; mats fold up and lock into place. The stage unfolds for storytelling and all types of performance. Smaller rooms, nooks, and alcoves—one of which can be a play kitchen or a village center—are visible from different perspectives.

1

1 *Rendering of auditorium*   **2** *Rendering of typical classroom*   **3** *Rendering of Bible Boulevard*

2

The Heavenly Hangout is a curved ribbon that children move along above the stage. The stage is flexible; the tower can stand in for Mount Sinai or the Tower of Babel and the backdrops can be easily modified. Stage hands, volunteers, and the technical crew become the *Promised Land* "carpenters," working together to create the passion and performance so critical to Turnpoint's teachings and mission.

Lining *Bible Boulevard*, each classroom takes its imagery from a biblical story, concept, or figure. The entries to each room are portals into thematic and age-appropriate design. As thresholds, these gateways contain iconographic elements, from a cutout of *Joseph's Coat of Many Colors* that children can stand behind, to *Noah's Ark* with a multitude of animals marching two by two. Cubbies for storage and coat hooks relate to the theme of each individual room and can be utilized front-side or for classroom purposes.

3

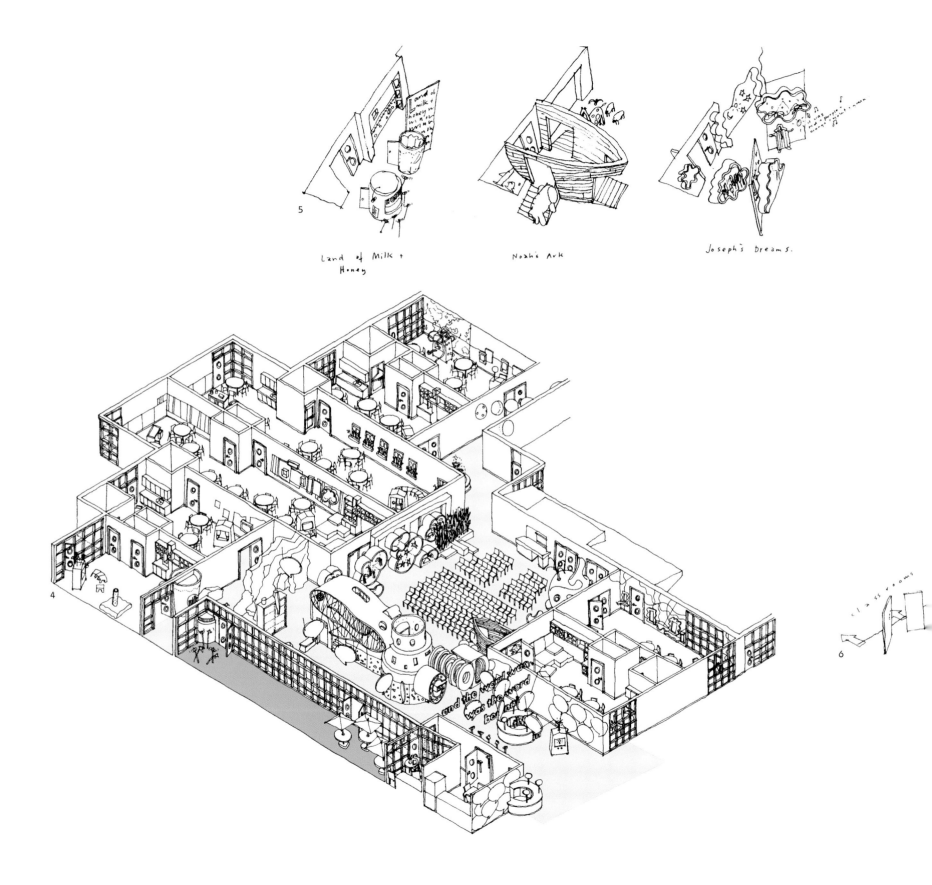

5

Land of Milk +
Honey

Noah's Ark

Joseph's Dreams.

4

and the word
was the word
begin

classrooms

6

4 *Rendering of the Promised Land*

5 *Design sketches of classroom thresholds*

6 *Design sketch of stage*   **7** *Plan layout*

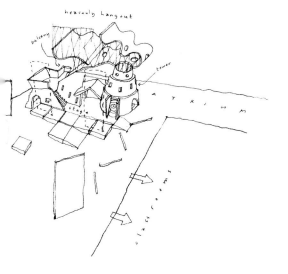

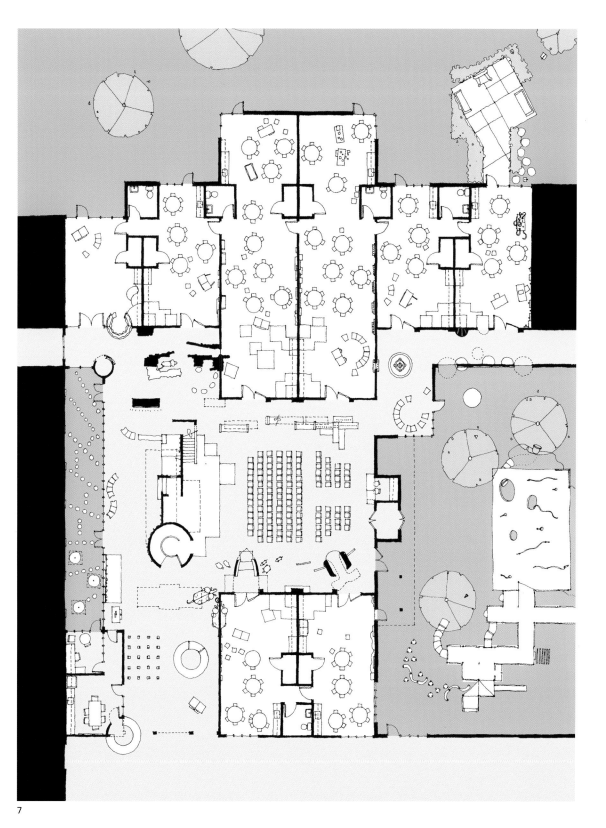

7

Multi-generational

Cybercafé
Chicago, Illinois

Designed specifically for high-school students, the *Cybercafé* learning center encourages interactive French-language acquisition. A dreary mezzanine was transformed into an appealing multimedia nook in which teens congregate. The *Cybercafé* is a sophisticated environment, akin to a hip café, where the richness of Francophone cultures is demonstrated through design and interaction.

Teens strolling in with overloaded backpacks settle in on the inviting L-shaped bench that safely stores possessions in cabinetry under the seat. Others move around the high-tech stools and teardrop tables, all on casters, effortlessly creating individual workstations or collaborative learning zones. During facilitated lessons, students gather together and afterwards rearrange themselves into small study groups. Since the *Cybercafé* was designed to take advantage of wireless technologies, laptops are brought along or checked out. The large LCD projection screen works with laptop connections and hooks into the cable

1

1 *High school study time* **2** *Design sketch*

2

connection for France's *TV 5*. Movable screens are dual-purpose: the fabric-covered side shades the room for projection, while the flip side is perfect for large-scale dry-erase use. A series of clocks with transparent faces, all set to Francophone nations, is superimposed on a large, write-on world map, an immediate atlas of global proportions.

Within the *Cybercafé*, there are multiple opportunities to record, research, show, speak, demonstrate, and share; all of which encourage teens to expand their horizons. Students create videos, perform hip-hop or Karaoke songs, virtually connect with other teens at Alliance sister schools, or take online tours of the Louvre. They are comfortable here because it has been designed with their input and with them in mind. The *Cybercafé* is an environment supportive of the practice of language skills while presenting opportunities to discover culture in ways that teens find relevant.

Architecture for Children Gallery
Art Institute of Chicago Chicago, Illinois

1 Concept sketch of playhouse entry   2 Gallery view   3 Playhouse detail

The architecture gallery at the Art Institute of Chicago is normally a solemn hallway. This exhibit presented an unusual opportunity to engage children and adults with a display of six architectural projects that had been constructed for use by children. The goal of the curatorial team, which included the design team, was to present these projects through models, drawings, photographs, and materials in ways that both children and adults would find captivating. Simple gestures further enhanced this goal. The design took its imagery from the way children draw, painting a line of blue down the hall for the sky, a stripe of green for the ground and then displaying the artwork between. For children, this created a zone on which to concentrate. For adults, the interpretives were consistent with the curatorial standards of the museum. A second set of labels was created to provoke children's inquiry as they looked at representations of each building. The fun, blue circles of information were spaced at child-height and moved across the gallery in rhythmic fashion.

1

2

The *Exploration Station*, one of the designer's architectural projects featured within the exhibit, inspired the exhibit's playhouse. An unusual, interactive element, the red-and-white-striped playhouse invited young museum-goers to move in and around it. Like a treasure hunt, children playfully discovered clues and artifacts, from metal wall panels to textured concrete flooring, from each of the exhibit's featured structures. A second comment book, placed on an accessible pedestal, was added. Like the labels, the book was designed to engage children about their architectural experience and museum visit.

3

Faces of Time

Chicago History Museum Chicago, Illinois

The installation for the traveling exhibit *Faces of Time* provided an element of intuitive interactivity attracting children and families to a history museum. Everyone has perhaps imagined himself or herself on the cover of *Time* magazine. With a larger-than-life *Time* cover as the gallery's entry portal, visitors became the latest cover story. This enticing, playful element drew children and families into the galleries, while introducing the content within.

Sequences of cover portraits were arranged both chronologically and thematically, grouping protagonists in often-provocative relationships, reflecting the news media. The exhibit creatively displayed 75 artworks, in various mediums, commissioned for the cover of the magazine and produced by many of the century's outstanding artists. The design and careful arrangement of *Faces of Time* helped illustrate and interpret the amazing accolade of being featured on the cover of *Time*.

Strong, graphic elements from *Time's* own venerable history inspired the gallery's bold backdrops of color and detail. ✍

1

2

4

1 *Putting yourself on a magazine cover*   2 *Concept sketch*   3,4 *Gallery views*

3

5 *Entry portal frames and informs visitors*   6 *Gallery view*

The bright red borders and oversized letters entice visitors and framed groupings of diverse subjects and media. Developed in collaboration with educators and program staff, a computer interactive created easy visitor access to the collection. Children and adults printed out cover stories from the full history of the magazine to read and take home. The combination of compelling imagery and storylines, along with the dynamic, hands-on design resulted in increased family attendance and unprecedented press coverage for this modestly sized traveling show.

6

7

8

10

12

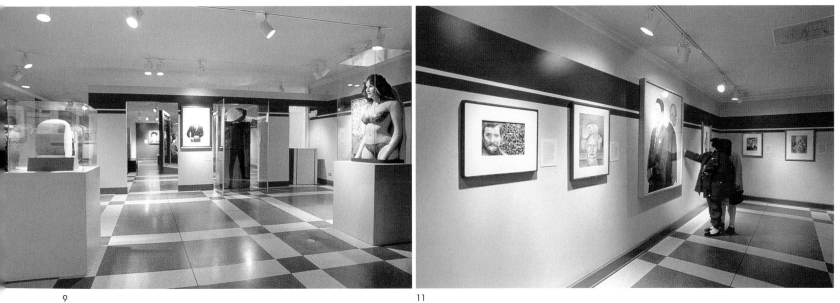

9

11

7–12 *Views of gallery installation*

A Force of Nature: The Life and Work of Jens Jensen

Chicago Cultural Center Chicago, Illinois

This rich environment brought to light the contributions of pioneering landscape architect Jens Jensen, developer of the Prairie style of landscape design. As Jensen used site to enhance design, this exhibit referentially interpreted his use of light, shadow, and color to create a forceful, natural exhibit of history and a place appropriate for a diverse, multi-age audience.

The soothing and elegant design solution referred strongly to Jensen's belief in nature as restorative to man's soul. Mini vistas, so critical in Jensen's environments, were created throughout, helping visitors become aware of their surroundings. The Midwestern palette was light and airy and energized the exhibit walls, murals, banners, and gateways. The *Force of Nature* entry was framed by a cutout graphic of a native tree, with its willowy branches adorning the slender portal. The exhibit areas were derived from Jensen's multiple roles: designer, conservationist, social reformer, planner, and artist. Elements of Jensen's work were utilized architecturally to create big panoramas

1

Please take one
and scatter
the seeds.

"WE OF TODAY DO HAVE IT WITHIN OUR POWER
TO BUILD A LIVABLE WORLD, BOTH FOR OURSELVES AND
FOR THOSE WHO FOLLOW US
SO THEY MIGHT INHERIT
A GOOD BEGINNING."

2

3

1 *Framing views of Jensen's landscapes*   2 *View of media gallery*   3 *View of council ring bench*

that displayed photographs, artifacts, and history. *Sun Openings*, used by Jensen to allow glimpses of sunlight to enter a space, were incorporated so that natural light filled the exhibit galleries. These slender openings drew visitors into the mini rooms that provided close-up views of Jensen's innovative work. A more theatrical approach to the exhibit was conveyed through the careful placement of large simulated Tecco Ware vases, dried native plants and foliage, and graphic ribbons of information.

Kitchen tables were provided so that families and school groups could sit, like Jensen did when working, to peruse artifacts and drawings. A series of painted slabs recreated the council ring concept, providing a contemplative place. Jensen often incorporated a circle of stones as a gathering place; these benches created mood, social interaction, and introspection. Children were invited to take home packets of native Midwestern seeds to plant, a reminder to propagate Jensen's love of the natural world. Visitors of all ages were inspired to recognize the importance of nature in their lives, were encouraged to help save Jensen landscapes, and were invited to acknowledge a great artist and designer.

5

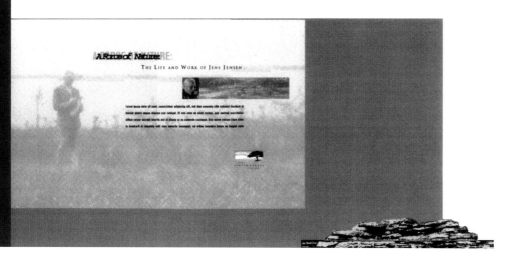

A Force of Nature: The Life and Work of Jens Jensen

7

6

Pear Design, Inc.

Chicago, Illinois

1 *Concept sketch* **Opposite** *View of "hello" entry* **3** *Colorful workstation*

Designers themselves, our colleagues at Pear Design Graphics demanded that their environment be expressive and reflect their design attitude and philosophy. With a move only a few weeks off, the new studio required a straightforward economical approach to both budget and schedule. By focusing on the essentials, extravagances of time, space, and materials were eliminated. In this way, economy informed design—streamlining, not inhibiting it.

An early envisioning session began with a big "hello," welcoming thoughts that appeared on an early sketch. These words instantly took hold as a graphic, dynamic concept. When visitors enter the suite, a "hello" wall graphic greets them and upon departure, the walls say "good-bye." Young children hand-painted the table and chairs that grace the entry hall, giving it a warm and familiar feel. The vivid color palette, applied through straightforward paint finishes, expresses an electric identity for the studio, which was also translated into collateral materials, from letterhead to brochures. ✍

1

3

A core of workstations provides low-walled nooks for staff, offering privacy while maintaining a visual connection. Two semi-private offices and a conference room were carved out for the principals.

Visitors comment that the new office literally glows. The efficient solution is elementary, expressive, and unexpected. The collaboration between designer and client-designer established a strong, holistic identity and branding that permeates environment, product, and service.

4,5 *Office views*

Informants for design

Informants for design: teaching, reflection, and inquiry

1 *The TR(i)Cycle*   **2** *Curating the iExhibit*   **3,4** *Views of the iExhibit gallery*

architectureisfun brings a core philosophy of educative design™ to every project. This ideology—design that educates as well as design that is fundamentally educated—is fulfilled through its participatory nature. Design educates by creating spaces for interactive play, learning, and self-discovery. Children gain knowledge about themselves and the world around them in creative and innovative ways. Design is educated through interactions with the user constituents during the planning and prototyping process. Collaboration sessions are held with local community members and creative sessions are held with children to educate the designers as to the needs and desires of those for whom the space is to be constructed. This helps create design that integrates pragmatic, developmental, and inspirational needs within the critical and distinct phases of childhood.

A TR(i)Cycle illustrates the methodology of educating design. The TR(i) acronym represents the teaching, reflecting, and inquiry that takes place as part of the design process. The (i) emphasizes the individual participant in both roles, as designer and as user of the design. The lower-case letter currently in vogue also references an association to many well-designed objects that children frequently use. The coincidence of the acronym and the cycle becomes a play on words for this metaphorical vehicle, the TR(i)Cycle. The metaphorical wheels—teaching, reflection, and inquiry—drive this design vehicle, but the riders (i) propel it. The wheels turn continually, representing cycles of growth, while referencing theories of learning.

1

Teaching is a rewarding, refreshing way to reconnect. Writing and speaking about design experiences, offering exploratory workshops for children, being an artist-in-residence, all keep one from becoming insolated. Engaging others in architectural dialogue forces a designer to synthesize past experiences and clarify personal philosophies.

Reflection is a necessary component for synthesis. It is through reflection that one is able to stop and consider

2

3   4

an experience—the successes, the failures, and the lessons—both learned and taught. Reflecting transforms experiences into knowledge that can be then utilized and propagated to other designers and students.

Inquiry is essential to educated design. In order to create spaces that are relevant to a particular audience, designers must seek a coherent view of the project. It is necessary to establish the expectations, requirements, and wishes of the intended audience. This can be done through an inquiry process of collaboration and observation. Yet, even with the most calculated inquiry process, gains cannot be made without the most essential component— that of listening.

Here are some of architectureisfun, Inc's pivotal experiences, exemplifying how to keep in touch with users of environments through educative design™.

iExhibit

The *iExhibit* offered middle-school age children a rare opportunity to impact, alter, and take responsibility for their environment through hands-on architecture. By building with oversized slotted card, children formed constructions, playrooms, or "museums," in which valued possessions were re-presented. Structural materials were easy enough to manipulate, large enough to create environments of stature, yet unstable enough to require cooperation in order to build. The dynamic of collaboration generated a growing awareness of the spatial environment as both individual and collective space.

As spontaneous architecture, the *iExhibit* was analogous to an architect's "charette," a design brainstorming session. Children utilized all available resources to creatively form structure and space. The *iExhibit* was intuitive and hands-on; design decisions were kid-made, allowing children to retain control over their work. Collecting and exhibiting were introduced as methods of interpretive design. Children could pre-select objects from their private possessions that they felt comprised a good collection. Creating exhibits, children came to understand that they have put not only their objects 🖐

on display, but also themselves. For those taking part in an impromptu architectural adventure, building was its own fun-filled journey. The *iExhibit* taught children in hands-on ways to visualize change and exercise informed choices—this made powerful architecture for kids.

Mies in America

For Chicago's Museum of Contemporary Art, a hands-on workshop based on the *Mies in America* exhibit was conceived. *Cozy Homes and Modernist Villas* afforded families an architectural exploration. In order that the "skin and bones construction" principle was understood, families reflected upon the master architect's style and body of work. They toured the galleries and explored steel high-rises and Mies' Barcelona Pavilion. Working with only cellophane, clay, and cardboard, children investigated transparency, proportion, and detail. A community of simple, yet elegant, platform homes arose, complete with Barcelona-style chairs and sculptural pools, all exemplifying the Miesian motto "less is more," but not forgetting that, as Venturi, Scott Brown & Izenour countered, "less is a bore," if you don't design with spirit and personality.

Walking Tour

School children can discover Chicago's architectural history on Loop Walking Tours. When teaching children about the built environment, it is necessary to help them build constructive vocabularies. To develop such sensibilities, children can explore the development of the city's architecture and plan firsthand—by hugging skyscrapers, touching walls, observing structures, and drawing sketches. Additionally, public school workshops can become ways for children to be introduced to the geometry of architecture, the history of their own neighborhoods, mapping, and to appreciate structures. For example, in an adapted *Building Experiences Trust* program, inner-city

5

6

7

children were introduced to the simplest structure within an elegant design solution by building tetrahedrons, alone and then collaboratively.

All of these experiences functioned as living laboratories. Children were taught about the built environment, how to speak about it, and how to express themselves through it. In sharing personal passions, the design team not only presented a learning opportunity for children, but also created an opportunity to learn from them. Watching children's interactions with various architectural elements and environments fulfilled the inquiry process. Lessons learned from these inquiries were reflected upon, so as to glean new knowledge applicable to our philosophy of educative design™.

In this cyclical process, educating through design serves to educate toward better design. When the child's voice is included in projects, a more educative and responsive environment is created, one that is specific to children's needs and wants. By implementing the model of the TR(i)Cycle, design becomes inclusive and better informed.

5 *Building a modernist villa at Mies in America*   **6** *Children in touch with Chicago architecture*   **7** *Learning to build*   **8,9** *Sketching Chicago architecture*

8

9

Building the dream

Materials, finishes, and furnishings appropriate for children

Designing for children carries a social responsibility beyond bright colors and scaled-down furnishings that only perceptive and informed grown-ups can understand.

There is a tendency to behave childishly when designing for children. Many designers believe it will be a straightforward activity filled with boisterous "young" clients and primary colors. In reality, it is an adult-sized job, rewarding to be sure, but filled with stringent constraints, from budget and schedule to federal guidelines on accessibility and requirements of educational mission. Still, we must strive to invest in our children's future; the creation of quality experience and environment must be the goal, which should be informed but not impeded by any set of constraints.

When designing for children, many of us are too simplistic. We recall our own childhoods and allow our own experiences to color the design. But today's child bears little resemblance to childhood in decades past. Design for today's children should not be cute or stylish. Children today are avid consumers, with sophisticated needs and mature outlooks. Their participation within the design process helps define and create relevant environments.

It takes more than a primary color palette and a few Lego™ blocks to make an environment for children.

We should design for children as we design for adults, only much, much better.

Design for children

- Meets pragmatic needs. It is inclusive. The needs of all become the foundation of good design.
- Meets developmental needs. It is age-appropriate, sensorial, comfortable, and communicative.
- Meets inspirational needs. It is beautiful. It is filled with wonder. It engages the senses and causes children to interact outside of themselves.
- Is relevant.

Blue sky materials, finishes, and furnishings

- Cross disciplines and borders to research materials for projects. Obsess about collecting catalogs, seeking out medical, technical, industrial, theatrical, and educational publications.
- Tune into the material, from the paraphernalia that accompanies a child's development from an infant to "teendom" to the multitude of design media and resources.

- Engage in "information-gathering"—collect data on whatever materials, furniture, activities, and environments are innovative, green, strangely wonderful, ergonomic, and educational.
- Reference child development and research educational theory; learn about Roger Hart, Howard Gardner, Rachel Carson, Louise Chawla, Richard Louv, Edith Cobb, and more.
- Ask children what they like. Look closely at what they buy, wear, play with, read, and watch.
- Test materials to see how they stand up to the constant attention of curious and creative youngsters.
- Mix economical everyday materials, juxtaposing the man-made and the natural, allowing them to converse.
- Find the potential in materials—look for resiliency, durability, flexibility, malleability, and longevity.
- Engage the intelligences through a world of sensorial materials, finishes, and furnishings.
- Color should match the experience, engaging visitors in experiential design.
- Prefer products that encourage an "I can do it myself" attitude. Creating open storage encourages "reach-ability" and "return-ability." Children intuitively know to put items back where they belong, creating accessibility and empowerment.
- Remember we are all multi-modal learners; we experience environments with different senses, and interpret them according to our own learning style.

Identify resources that can be entrusted to environments that support learning and play—categorizing solutions via pragmatic, developmental, and inspirational criteria.

Rationales for materials

Pragmatics	Developmentals	Inspirationals
Welcoming – Invitational	Sensorial	Beautiful
Safe	Independent	Colorful
Accessible	Friendly	Graphic
Sustainable	Age-appropriate	Natural
Inclusive	Authentic	Textural
Economic	Hands-on	Usual – Unusual
Durable	Interpretive	Pattern – Rhythm
Standard (non-custom) – Custom (non-standard)	Thematic	Familiar – Unfamiliar
Multipurpose	Reassuring	Visionary
Multi-generational	"Smart" (multiple intelligent)	Wet
Malleable	Intuitive	Recycled – Reused
Resilient	Tactile	Ordered – Grid
Resistant	Responsibility	Referential – Respectful
Flexible	Multi-sensory (olfactory, visual, auditory, etc.)	Perspective
Tested (prototyped)	Comfortable – Spacious	Kinetic – Static
Sound-absorbing (acoustical properties)	Communicative	Malleable
Clean	Legible	Symbolic – Iconic
Timely	Relevant	Funny, humorous, quirky
INFORMATIVE	SCALE	SCALE
SCALE	OPERATIONAL	OPERATIONAL
EDUCATIONAL AND PLAYFUL	EDUCATIONAL AND PLAYFUL	EDUCATIONAL AND PLAYFUL
FUN	**FUN**	**FUN**

Bright stripes cheer open, well-used entry

Economic

Comfortable – Spacious

Colorful

(Forbo Linoleum: Marmoleum)

Walk or wheel-in accessible interactive window

Accessible

Operational

Usual – Unusual

(Armstrong: Excelon VCT)

Waterjet cut carpet tiles

Durable

Legible

Pattern

(Lees Carpets: NeoFloor)

Matting used on wall for acoustical and textural properties

Acoustical

Sensorial

Ordered – Grid

(C/S Group: Duromat)

Extra-wide, patterned hallway for teaching and circulation

Multipurpose

Reassuring

Familiar – Unfamiliar

(Interface Flooring Systems: modular pop shapes)

Intimate walled space for family interaction

Multi-generational

Reassuring

Familiar – Unfamiliar

(JM Lynne: Sincol E wallcovering)

Dry-erase graffiti surface

Resistant

Age-appropriate

Educational and playful

(MDC Wallcoverings: Memerase)

Linking stools teamed with custom carts

Standard custom

Responsibility

Malleable

(Educational Furniture: Kinderlink stools)

Peephole in reading tree

Safe

Fun

Perspective

(Abet Laminati: graphic laminates)

Recycled fencing surrounds artist façade

Sustainable

Educational and playful

Recycled – Reused

(American Recycled Plastic, Inc.: recycled fence and lumber)

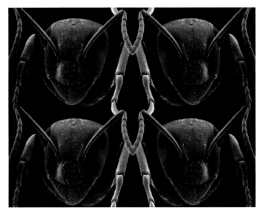

Microscopic photography turned into surfacing

Informative

Interpretive

Symbolic – Iconic

(Wilsonart Laminate: custom Dennis Kunkel digital print on laminate)

Scaled speaker tubes with custom metal otter trellis

Resilient

Communicative

Scale

(Landscape Structures, Inc.: Speaker Talk Tubes)

Product information

Furniture

BioFit Engineered Products
PO Box 109
Waterville, OH 43566
Web: www.biofit.com
Products: laboratory furniture and stools

Community Playthings
359 Gibson Hill Road
Chester, NY 10918
Email: sales@communityplaythings.com
Web: www.communityplaythings.com
Products: children's furniture and systems

Educational Furniture Inc.
5 Alden Street, Suite 7
Cranford, NJ 07016
Email: info@efurnitureinc.com
Web: www.kinderlink.com
Products: Kinderlinks linking stools

Fatboy USA, LLC.
PO Box 400
5201 AK's-Hertogenbosch
The Netherlands
Email: info@fatboy.nl
Web: www.fatboy.nl
Products: bean bags

Gressco Ltd.
328 Moravian Valley Road
Waunakee, WI 53597
Email: info@gresscoltd.com
Web: www.gresscoltd.com
Products: children's and library

Haba
Habermaass Corporation
PO Box 42
Skanaeteles, NY 13152-9371
Email: info@habausa.com
Web: www.haba.de
Products: children's and play equipment

Herman Miller
PO Box 302
Zeeland, MI 49464-0302
Email: info@hermanmiller.com
Web: www.hermanmiller.com

Knoll
222 Merchandise Mart Plaza, Suite 1111
Chicago, IL 60654
Email: mfredy@knoll.com
Web: www.knoll.com

Knothead Furniture Showroom
314 W. Institute Place
Chicago, IL 60610
Email: jbone@landonbonebaker.com
Web: www.landonbonebaker/knothead
Products: furniture

Maine Cottage Furniture

PO Box 935

Yarmouth, ME 04096

Email: customerservice@mainecottage.com

Web: www.mainecottage.com

Products: furniture

Furniture and designed objects

Kartell

39 Greene Street

New York, NY 10013

Email: jryan@kartellus.com

Web: www.kartell.it

Magis

Via Magnadola

15 – 31045 Motta di Livenza

Treviso, Italy

Email: info@magisdesign.com

Web: www.magisdesign.com

Topdeq

3 Security Drive, Suite 303

Cranbury, NJ 08512

Web: www.topdeq.com

Unica

7540 Dean Martin Drive, Suite 501

Las Vegas, NV 89139

Email: info@unica.com

Web: www.unicahome.com

Site furnishings, green screen, and signage

American Recycled Plastics, Inc.

1500 Main Street

Palm Bay, FL 32905

Email: plasticlumber@hotmail.com

Web: www.itsrecycled.com

Products: fencing – plastics and lumber

Dura Art Stone

11010 Live Oak

Fontana, CA 92337

Email: fontana@duraartstone.com

Web: www.duraartstone.com

Products: landscape furniture

Gemini Letters and Signs

128 South Bolton Street

Marlborough, MA 01752

Email: sales@geminisignletters.com

Web: www.geminisignletters.com

Products: signage

Greenscreen

1743 La Cienega Boulevard

Los Angeles, CA 90035

Email: info@greenscreen.com

Web: www.greenscreen.com

Products: green screen systems and panels

Hi Spy Viewing Machines

9124 Racetrack Road

RR #6 Cobourg, Ontario

Canada K9A 4J9

Email: rod@hispyviewing.com

Web: www.hispyviewing.com

Products: viewing machines

Keystone Ridge

PO Box 2008

Butler, PA 16003

Email: info@keystoneridge.com

Web: www.keystoneridgedesigns.com

Products: children's and adult outdoor furniture

RPI

7079 Peck Road

Marlette, MI 48453

Email: rpi@rpiweb.com

Web: www.rpiweb.com

Playground and recreational equipment

Carron Net

623 17th Street

Two Rivers, WI 54241

Email: sales@carronnet.com

Web: www.carronnet.com

Products: safety netting

Earthscapes Play Structures

217 Murphy Avenue

Ferguson, KY 42533

Email: es@earthscapestructures.com

Web: www.earthscapestructures.com

Products: playground components and equipment (recycled)

Kompan

7717 New Market Street

Olympia, WA 98501

Email: info@kompan.com

Web: www.kompan.com

Products: playground equipment

Landscape Structures Inc.

601 7th Street South

Delano, MN 55328

Web: www.playlsi.com

Products: playground equipment

Pyramide USA, Inc.

15829 Temple Hall Lane

Leesburg, VA 20176

Email: info@climbpyramide.com

Web: www.climbpyramide.com

Products: climbing systems

SoftPlay, LLC.
12100 Vance Davis Drive
Charlotte, NC 28269
Email: softplay@softplay.com
Web: www.softplay.com
Products: playground equipment

Lighting

Arte de Mexico
1000 Chestnut Street
Burbank, CA 91506
Email: sales@artedemexico.com
Web: www.artedemexico.com

Artemide
223 West Erie Street
Chicago, IL 60610
Email: info@artemide.com
Web: www.artemide.us

Baselight Corporation
177 Atlantic Street
Pomona, CA 91768
Email: sales@baselight.com
Web: www.baselight.com
Products: arbor and miscellaneous fixtures

Color Kinetics
10 Milk Street, Suite 1100
Boston, MA 02108
Email: info@colorkinetics.com
Web: www.colorkinetics.com
Products: iColor coves

Eureka Lighting
225, De Liége Quest, #200
Montreal, Quebec
Canada H2P 1H4
Email: info@eurekalighting.com
Web: www.eurekalighting.com

Expo Design Inc.
105-A Glen Street
Glen Cove, NY 11542
Email: info@expodesigninc.com
Web: www.expodesigninc.com
Products: Swarm chandeliers

Halo, Cooper Lighting
400 Busse Road
Elk Grove Village, IL 60007
Email: info@cooperlighting.com
Web: www.cooperlighting.com

Lamplight Designs Inc.
117 North Spring Street
Mason, TX 76856
Email: info@lamplightdesigns.com
Web: www.lamplightdesigns.com
Products: chandeliers

Lite Control
100 Hawks Avenue
Hanson, MA 02341
Email: info@litecontrol.com
Web: www.litecontrol.com
Products: MOD pendant fixtures

Luraline Lighting
Exciting Products Manufacturing Corp.
2388 Northwest 150th Street
Opa Locka, FL 33054
Email: salesandcustomerservice@luraline.com
Web: www.luraline.com

Rosco U.S.
52 Harbor View
Stamford, CT 06902
Email: info@rosco.com
Web: www.rosco.com
Products: theatrical

Floors

Amtico International Inc.
6480 Roswell Road
Atlanta, GA 30328
Email: samples@amtico.com
Web: www.amtico.com
Products: Innovation line

Armstrong World Industries, Inc.
PO Box 3001
Lancaster, PA 17604
Email: cschieren@armstrong.com
Web: www.armstrong.com
Products: vinyl composite tile (VCT)

EcoSurfaces Commercial Flooring
c/o Gerbert Limited
PO Box 4944
Lancaster, PA 17604
Email: info@ecosurfaces.com
Web: www.ecosurfaces.com
Products: green

Expanko
3135 Lower Valley Road
Parkesburg, PA 19365
Email: sales@expanko.com
Web: www.expanko.com
Products: rubber – green

Interface
440 N. Wells
Chicago, IL 60610
Email: joe.foley@us.interface.inc.com
Web: www.interfaceinc.com
Products: carpet tile

Lees Carpets
500 TownPark Lane, Suite #400
Kennesaw, GA 30144
Email: info@leescarpets.com
Web: www.leescarpets.com
Products: NeoFloor carpet tile and broadloom

Plynyl
Chilewich LLC
44 East 32nd Street
New York, NY 10016
Email: info@chilewich.com
Web: www.chilewich.com
Products: flooring – woven, vinyl

Saltillo Tile Company
2731 Cerrillos Road
Santa Fe, NM 87507
Email: info@saltillotilecompany.com
Web: www.saltillotilecompany.com
Products: Mexican and Spanish tiles

Floor and walls

Bisazza Tile
3540 NW 72nd Avenue
Miami, FL 33122
Email: info@bisazzausa.com
Web: www.bisazzausa.com

C/S Companies
499 Col. Eileen Collins Boulevard
Syracuse, NY 13212
Email: contactus@cscos.com
Web: www.cscos.com
Products: DuroMat (used as wall surface)

Florida Tile
320 West Main Street
Lakeland, FL 33815
Email. salesdept@floridatile.com
Web: www.floridatile.com
Products: wall/floor tile

Forbo Linoleum Inc.
Humboldt Industrial Park
PO Box 667
US-Hazleton, PA 18201
Email: info@fl.na.com
Web: www.forbolinoleumna.com
Products: Marmoleum, Artoleum, bulletin board

Globus Cork
741 E. 136th Street
Bronx, NY 10454
Email: info@corkfloor.com
Web: www.corkfloor.com
Products: floor/wall surfaces

Holo-Walls
5594 Shadow Canyon
Westlake Village, CA 91362
Email: litefx@aol.com
Web: www.holowalls.com
Products: holographic wall surfacing and floor surfacing

Johnsonite
16910 Munn Road
Chagrin Falls, OH 44023
Email: info@johnsonite.com
Web: www.johnsonite.com
Products: floor/wall surfaces

Walls

Florida Tile
320 West Main Street
Lakeland, FL 33815
Email: salesdept@floridatile.com
Web: www.floridatile.com
Products: tile – wall/floor surfaces

Innovations in Wall Coverings, Inc.
10–148 Merchandise Mart
Chicago, IL 60654
Email: cranvik@innovationsusa.com
Web: www.innovationsusa.com
Products: fabrics, wall coverings ("green" products)

JM Lynne Wall Covering
200 Varick Street, 8th floor
New York, NY 10014
Web: www.jmlynne.com
Products: wallcoverings

MDC Wallcovering
1200 Arthur Avenue
Elk Grove Village, IL 60007
Email: info@mdcwall.com
Web: www.mdcwall.com
Products: wallcovering – Memerase (dry-erase wallcovering)

Panelite U.S.
3341 S. LaCienega Place
Los Angeles, CA 90016
Email: info@panelite.us
Web: www.panelite.us

Pinscreen Components
Children's Discovery Museum of San Jose
180 Woz Way
San Jose, CA 95110
Email: pinscreen@cdm.prg
Web: www.cdm.org
Products: pinscreen interactive panels

Questech Metals
92 Park Street
Rutland, VT 05701
Email: info@questechmetals.com
Web: www.questechmetals.com
Products: tile

Sandhill Industries, Inc.
6898 S. Supply Way, Suite 100
Boise, ID 83716
Email: sales@sandhillind.com
Web: www.sandhillind.com
Product: glass tile 100% recycled

Summitville Tile
1101 Lunt Avenue
Elk Grove Village, IL 60001
Email: info@summitville.com
Web: www.summitville.com
Products: quarry tile and more

Wolf Gordon
Merchandise Mart #10–161
200 World Trade Center
Chicago, IL 60654
Email: info@wolf-gordon.com
Web: www.wolf-gordon.com
Products: wallcovering

Yemm & Hart
1417 Madison 308
Marquand, MO 63655
Email: info@yemmhart.com
Web: www.yemmhart.com
Products: plastics and rubber (recycled)

Ceilings

Tectum Inc.
PO Box 3002
Newark, OH 43058
Email: info@tectum.com
Web: www.tectum.com
Products: acoustical/ceiling systems – panels

USG Interiors, Inc.
125 South Franklin Street
Chicago, IL 60606
Email: samplit@usg.com
Web: www.usg.com
Products: ceiling systems – Topo 3-dimensional system

Paint

Benjamin Moore & Company
51 Chestnut Ridge Road
Montvale, NJ 07645
Email: info@benjaminmoore.com
Web: www.benjaminmoore.com
Products: paint and stains

Cabot Stains
100 Hale Street
Newburyport, MA 01950
Email: scarrona@cabotstain.com
Web: www.cabotstains.com

Pratt & Lambert
20677 Swans Way
Deer Park, IL 60010
Email: info@prattandlambert.com
Web: www.prattandlambert.com

Laminate and metal

ABET Inc.
60 West Sheffield Avenue
Englewood, NJ 07631
Email: usa@abetlaminati.com
Web: www.abetlaminati.com
Products: laminate – Tefor "green" products

McNichols
5505 West Gray Street
Tampa, FL 33609
Email: sales@mcnichols.com
Web: www.mcnichols.com
Products: metal products – mesh

Wilsonart
14822 S. Ellis
Dolton, IL 60419
Email: info@wilsonart.com
Web: www.wilsonart.com
Products: laminate

Wood and millwork

American Recycled Plastics, Inc.
1500 Main Street
Palm Bay, FL 32905
Email: plasticlumber@hotmail.com
Web: www.itsrecycled.com
Products: fencing – plastics and recycled lumber

Kirei USA
1805 Newton Avenue
San Diego, CA 92113
Email: info@kireiusa.com
Web: www.kireiusa.com
Products: flooring – bamboo ("green" products)

Mountain Lumber
PO Box 289
Ruckersville, VA 22968
Email: sales@mountainlumber.com
Web: www.mountainlumber.com
Products: re-milled salvaged lumber

TerraMai

PO Box 696

McCloud, CA 96057

Web: www.terramai.com

Hardware

Equipto, A Division of Consolidated Storage Companies, Inc.

225 Main Street

Tatamy, PA 18085

Email: customerservice@equipto.com

Web: www.equipto.com

Products: shelving and hardware

Hafele America Co.

3901 Cheyenne Drive

Archdale, NC 27263

Web: www.hafele.com

Products: hardware

Kee Industrial Products, Inc.

100 Stradtman Street

Buffalo, NY 14206

Email: info@keeklamp.com

Web: www.keeklamp.com

Products: Kee Klamp

McMaster-Carr

PO Box 740100

Atlanta, GA 30374

Email: atl.sales@mcmaster.com

Web: www.mcmaster.com

Products: hardware – industrial supplies

Outerwater Plastics

4 Passaic Street

Wood-Ridge, NJ 07075

Web: www.outerwater.com

Products: industrial supplies – hardware and miscellaneous

W.W. Grainger, Inc.

829 N. Orleans

Chicago, IL 60610

Email: info@grainger.com

Web: www.grainger.com

Products: hardware and industrial supplies

West Marine

PO Box 50070

Watsonville, CA 95077

Email: customercare@westmarine.com

Web: www.westmarine.com

Products: industrial supplies – hardware

Fabrics

Architex International

3333 Commercial Avenue

Northbrook, IL 60062

Email: architex@architex-ljh.com

Web: www.architex-ljh.com

Products: fabric

Dazian Fabrics

PO Box 2121

Secaucus, NJ 07096

Web: www.dazian.com

Products: theatrical supplies – fabric, drapery, and ChromaKey

DesignTex, A Steelcase Company

200 Varick Street

New York, NY 10014

Email: info@designtex.com

Web: www.designtex.com

Products: fabric and upholstery

Garrett Leather

1360 Niagara Street

Buffalo, NY 14213

Email: info@garrettleather.com

Web: www.garrettleather.com

Products: fabric – leather

Knoll

222 Merchandise Mart Plaza, Suite 1111

Chicago, IL 60654

Email: mfredy@knoll.com

Web: www.knoll.com

Products: furniture, fabrics

Maharam

Merchandise Mart, Suite 1188

Chicago, IL 60654

Email: clientservices@maharam.com

Web: www.maharam.com

Products: fabrics – Charles and Ray Eames, Hella Jongerius, Alexander Girard

Naugahyde

290 Coconut Avenue, Suite 1-A

Sarasota, FL 34236

Email: info@naugahyde.com

Web: www.naugahyde.com

Products: fabric – vinyl

Rose Brand

75 Ninth Avenue

New York, NY 10011

Email: customerservice@rosebrand.com

Web: www.rosebrand.com

Products: theatrical supplies – drapery

Miscellaneous resources

Special needs

Abilitations
3155 Northwoods Parkway
Norcross, GA 30071
Email: customer.service@sportime.com
Web: www.abilitations.com
Products: special needs equipment

EnableMart Technology For Everyone
4210 East 4th Plain Boulevard
Vancouver, WA 98661
Email: sales@enablemart.com
Web: www.enablemart.com
Products: assistive technology and more

FlagHouse
601 FlagHouse Drive
Hasbrouck Heights, NJ 07604-3116
Email: sales@flaghouse.com
Web: www.flaghouse.com
Products: assistive technology and equipment for
physical and developmental disabilities

Educational supplies and learning toys

Acorn Naturalists
155 El Camino Real
Tustin, CA 92780
Email: emailacorn@aol.com
Web: www.acornnaturalists.com
Products: nature-related educational resources

American Science and Surplus
PO Box 1030
Skokie, IL 60076
Email: service@sciplus.com
Web: www.sciplus.com
Products: educational supplies – science-related
products

Barnard, Ltd.
375 W. Erie
Chicago, IL 60610
Email: www.themedecor.com
Web: www.themedecor.com
Products: food replicas

Brodart Library Supplies
280 North Road
Clinton County Industrial Park
McElhatten, PA 17748
Email: furniture@brodart.com
Web: www.brodart.com
Products: library furnishings and supplies

Edmund Industrial Optics
101 East Gloucester Pike
Barrington, NJ 08007
Email: sales@edmundoptics.com
Web: www.edmundoptics.com
Products: laboratory objects – optical parts and
supplies

Edmund Scientific
60 Pearce Avenue
Tonawanda, NY 14150
Email: scientifics@edsci.com
Web: www.scientificsonline.com
Products: educational supplies – laboratory objects,
magnets

Environments Inc.
PO Box 1348
Beaufort, SC 29901
Email: environments@eichild.com
Web: www.eichild.com
Products: educational supplies

Fisher Science Education
4500 Turnberry Drive, Suite A
Hanover Park, IL 60133
Email: info@fisheredu.com
Web: www.fisheredu.com
Products: educational supplies – furniture,
scientific, laboratory

Flag House
601 FlagHouse Drive
Hasbrouck Heights, NJ 07604
Email: customerservice@flaghouse.com
Web: www.flaghouse.com
Products: educational supplies

Frey Scientific Catalog
PO Box 8101
Mansfield, OH 44903
Email: customercare@freyscientific.com
Web: www.freyscientific.com
Products: educational supplies

Lab Safety Supply
PO Box 1368
Janesville, WI 53547
Email: custsvc@labsafety.com
Web: www.labsafety.com
Products: laboratory objects – safety

Lakeshore Learning
2695 E. Dominguez Street
Carson, CA 90895
Email: info@lakeshorelearning.com
Web: www.lakeshorelearning.com
Products: educational supplies

Learning Curve
1111 W. 22nd Street, Suite 320
Oak Brook, IL 60523
Email: cs@learningcurve.com
Web: www.learningcurve.com
Products: educational supplies – learning toys

Markertek
PO Box 397
Saugerties, NY 12477
Email: sales@markertek.com
Web: www.markertek.com
Products: AV equipment

Nasco Arts & Crafts
PO Box 901
Fort Atkinson, WI 53538
Email: custserv@enasco.com
Web: www.enasco.com
Products: arts and crafts

Play Fair Toys
1690 28th Street
Boulder, CO 80301
Email: service@playfairtoys.com
Web: www.playfairtoys.com

Rhode Island Novelty
19 Industrial Lane
Johnston, RI 02919
Email: info@rinovelty.com
Web: www.rinovelty.com
Products: party supplies – novelties

School Specialty
W6316 Design Drive
Greenville, WI 54942
Email: info@schoolspecialty.com
Web: www.schoolspecialty.com
Products: educational supplies

Decorative accessories and display props

Clippership Shop
PO Box 656
Amherst, MA 01004
Email: info@clippershipdistribution.com
Web: www.clippershipdistribution.com
Products: Chinese kites and decorative objects

Cosanti
6433 E. Doubletree Ranch Road
Paradise Valley, AZ 85253
Email: cosanti@qwest.net
Web: www.cosanti.com
Products: designed objects – wind chimes

Fake-Foods.com
204 North El Camino Real, #432
Encinitas, CA 92024
Email: information@fake-foods.com
Web: www.fake-foods.com
Products: decorative items – food replicas

Hubert
9555 Dry Fork Road
Harrison, OH 45030
Email: info@hubert.com
Web: www.hubert.com
Products: display objects

Native American Expressions
19414 E. Highway 6
Alvin, TX 77511
Email: nae@nativeamericanexpressions.net
Web: www.nativeamericanexpressions.net
Products: Native American artifacts – dream catchers, etc.

Artisans, craftsmen, and specialty fabricators

Gulley Studio
6 High Street
Williamsport, IN 47993
Email: info@gulleystudio.com
Web: www.gulleystudio.com
Specialty fabricator: models, specimens

Dennis Kunkel
PO Box 2008
Kailua, HI 96734
Email: kunkel@denniskunkel.com
Web: www.denniskunkel.com
Specialty fabricator: microscopic photographs (used to create custom laminates)

LaBrosse, Ltd.
2603 W. Barry Avenue
Chicago, IL 60618
Email: info@labrosseltd.com
Web: www.labrosseltd.com
Specialty fabricator: children's environments – interactive elements

Luckey & Company
165 Short Beach Road
Branford, CT 06405
Email: info@luckeyclimbers.com
Web: www.luckeyclimbers.com
Specialty fabricator: climbing systems

Alejandro Romero
3121 N. Rockwell Street
Chicago, IL 60618
Web: www.rogallery.com
Specialty fabricator: mosaic artist

Sound Play
PO Box 115
Parrott, GA 31777
Email: bond@soundplay.com
Web: www.soundplay.com
Specialty fabricator: children's interactive sound elements

Taylor Studios
1320 Harmon Drive
Rantoul, IL 61866
Web: www.taylorstudios.com
Specialty fabricator: museum exhibits

Project credits

Architectural

DuPage Children's Museum

Design architect	architectureisfun, Inc.
Architect of record	Nagle Hartray Danker Kagan McKay Penney Architects Planners
Exhibit architect	architectureisfun, Inc.
Exhibit design	MindSplash (Creativity Connections)
Photographer	Doug Snower Photography
Client	DuPage Children's Museum Naperville, Illinois

Exploration Station Children's Museum and Community Center

Design architect	architectureisfun, Inc.
Architect of record	Moline Design Group
Exhibit architecture	architectureisfun, Inc.
Photographer	Doug Snower Photography
Client	Exploration Station Children's Museum and Community Center Bourbonnais, Illinois

Kidscommons

Design architect and exhibit design	architectureisfun, Inc.
Exhibit developer and graphic designer	Chermayeff and Geismar
Exhibit architect	architectureisfun, Inc.
Photographer	Doug Snower Photography
Client	Kidscommons Columbus, Indiana

The Children's Grove

Exhibit architect	architectureisfun, Inc.
Landscape architect	Lake County Forest Preserves
Photographer	Peter Exley, FAIA
Client	Lake County Forest Preserves Independence Grove Libertyville, Illinois

Eastern Maine Children's Museum

Exhibit architect	architectureisfun, Inc.
Client	Eastern Maine Children's Museum Bangor, Maine

Mid-Michigan Children's Museum

Exhibit architect	architectureisfun, Inc.
Exhibit developer	Mary Sinker
Graphic design	Pear Design Inc.
Model fabricator	Michael Machnic
Model photographer	Doug Snower Photography
Client	Mid-Michigan Children's Museum Saginaw, Michigan

The Children's Museum

Exhibit architect architectureisfun, Inc.

Exhibit developer Mary Sinker

Graphic design Pear Design Inc.

Model fabricator Adrian Ferguson, Urban Alchemy, LLC

Model photographer Doug Snower Photography

Client The Children's Museum Greenville, South Carolina

Out-of-doors

Rediscovering Nature: Kids Can Dig It

Architect and author architectureisfun, Inc.

Ogden Park Regional Playground

Exhibit architect and interactive design architectureisfun, Inc.

Landscape architect Wolff Clements Landscape Architecture

Photographer Doug Snower Photography

Client City of Chicago Park District Chicago Illinois

Winnetka Public School Nursery Outdoor Learning Environment

Architect and exhibit architect architectureisfun, Inc.

Photographer Doug Snower Photography

Client Winnetka Public School Nursery Winnetka, Illinois

Bonner Heritage Farm

Interior architect, exhibit architect, interpretive design architectureisfun, Inc.

Historic architect Carow Architects

Fabricator Exhibit Works

Artists– Tornado Sculpture Stuart Keeler and Michael Machnic

Photographer Doug Snower Photography

Client Bonner Heritage Farm, Lake County Forest Preserves Lindenhurst, Illinois

Texas A&M Math and Science Education Center at Corpus Christi

Exhibit architect and interpretive design architectureisfun, Inc.

Architect of record Durrant Group

Client Texas A&M University Corpus Christi, Texas

Experiential

Playmaze

Interior architect and exhibit architect architectureisfun, Inc.

Computer programs Raul Silva Digital Media and architectureisfun, Inc.

Fabricator LaBrosse, Ltd.

Photographer Doug Snower Photography

Client Chicago Children's Museum Chicago, Illinois

The Stinking Truth About Garbage

Interior Architect, exhibit architect, interpretive design architectureisfun, Inc.

Computer programs Raul Silva Digital Media and architectureisfun, Inc.

Fabricator Proto Productions & Taylor Studios

Photographer 1 Doug Snower Photography

Photographer 2 Steve Kagan (image of children at façade)

Client Chicago Children's Museum Chicago, Illinois

Medieval Castle

Interior architect and exhibit architect architectureisfun, Inc.

Photographer Doug Snower Photography

Client Exploration Station Children's Museum and Community Center Bourbonnais, Illinois

Kidzone

Interior architect and exhibit architect architectureisfun, Inc.

Fabricator LaBrosse, Ltd.

Photographer Doug Snower Photography

Client Louisville Science Center Louisville, Kentucky

My Museum

Exhibit architect and exhibit developer architectureisfun, Inc.

Exhibit developer Chicago Children's Museum

Fabricator LaBrosse, Ltd.

Photographer Doug Snower Photography

Client Chicago Children's Museum Chicago, Illinois

Adventure With Babar, King of the Elephants

Exhibit architect and exhibit developer architectureisfun, Inc.

Exhibit developer Chicago Children's Museum

Client Chicago Children's Museum and Nelvana Ltd.

Alice in Wonderland Play Space

Exhibit architect architectureisfun, Inc.

Artist Deloss McGraw

Client Young At Art Children's Museum Davie, Florida

Acknowledgments

Emma Exley serendipitously instigated our professional path. This entire portfolio is touched by shared experiences with our daughter and her inspiration and critique. Emma is our most important work and the recipient of our grateful acknowledgment.

We became conscious of the need for good design for children as fledgling parents —and found ourselves supporting venues valued by our daughter. Enormous gratitude should go to the Chicago Children's Museum and the Exploration Station, who were brave, visionary and supportive of our shift from museum volunteers to designers of environments for children as a full-time venture. Louise Belmont Skinner and Marilyn O'Flaherty, in particular, nurtured our early goals and aligned them to create a wonderful fit for their projects.

Innovative, paradigm-shaping projects are born from visionary clients. We are grateful to all of our clients and the friendship our collaborations have yielded alongside these projects.

Formative and influential experiences were enjoyed in the apprenticeship of the offices of Skidmore, Owings and Merrill in Chicago, London, and Boston. Likewise, an unbelievable opportunity offered by Robert Venturi, Denise Scott Brown, and Steven Izenour in the office of Venturi Scott Brown and Associates enriched the experience of a graduate student at the University of Pennsylvania. VSBA encouraged our perspectives on design in many new ways—that our work has meaning and wit, that it is relevant—much comes from the realizations, precedents, and observations made in that Philadelphia office.

The following mentors and peers are recognized for their impact upon our lives and our practice:

Annette Baldwin, Tom Brock and Kelly Ducheny, Odile Compagnon, Weld Coxe, Mark Dytham, May Hawfield, Drea Howenstein, Anthony Hurtig, Don Kalec, Roger Kallman, Blair Kamin, John Kelly, Astrid Klein, Tom Larsen, Pete Landon, Christopher Lee, Giles and Connie Moore, Anders Nereim, Angela Paterakis, Joan Pomaranc, Grace Kulklinski Rappe and Scott Rappe, Mark Schaefer, Alice Sinkevitch, Richard Solomon, Constantine Vasilios and Anna Nowobilski, Dan Vieyra, Brian Wall, Jim Zahn, and Tom Zurowski.

We recognize the essential and enthusiastic contributions of past and current collaborators:

Shalini Agrawal, Amy Batchu, Miguel Canon, Meredith Corbett, Adrian Ferguson, Adya Kashuba, Kelly Lovell, Nicole Miller, Alan Salabert, Doug Snower, and Sudie Wentling. Also, Thorsten Boesch, Nick Glazebrook, Linda Jackson, Norbert Marszalek, Jeff Smiejek, Tony LaBrosse, Pam Parker, and the artists at LaBrosse, Ltd.

In a practice that focuses on family, the precedents set by our own parents and siblings deserve special recognition. We are grateful for their influences.

Peter and Sharon Exley